WORLD CHRISTIAN BOOKS NO. 6

THE CHRISTIAN CHARACTER

World Christian Books

A SERIES OF BOOKS COVERING THE WHOLE RANGE
OF THE CHRISTIAN FAITH IN THE MODERN WORLD

Edited by Bishop Stephen Neill

*Sponsored by the International Missionary Council
in co-operation with the Christian Literature
Council of Great Britain and the Committee on
World Literacy and Christian Literature of the
United States, and published by the United Society
for Christian Literature and the Lutterworth Press,
London.*

WORLD CHRISTIAN BOOKS
No. 6

THE CHRISTIAN CHARACTER

by

S T E P H E N   N E I L L

UNITED SOCIETY FOR CHRISTIAN LITERATURE
LUTTERWORTH PRESS
LONDON

First published 1955

The Scripture quotations in this book are from the Revised Standard Version of the Bible; except a few, marked R.V., which are from the English Revised Version.

Printed by Page Bros. (Norwich) Ltd.
Mile Cross Lane, Norwich

Preface by the General Editor

The beginning of the twentieth century was a period of hope for the Christian Church. The western Churches appeared strong and rich, and great new Churches were growing quickly in almost all parts of the world. It seemed that the Gospel might spread through the whole earth without meeting serious opposition. Fifty years later all is changed. Every Christian knows that these are hard days for the Church. The old faiths are taking on new life and new power of resistance to the Gospel. New faiths, such as communism, are attracting millions of believers. Christians are convinced that Jesus Christ is the last Word of God to man, and that all the future is in His hands; but they know also that the Faith cannot survive and grow unless Churches and individuals receive new life, new confidence and new power to witness. In these days every Christian must be an evangelist.

To-day it is not enough to believe—it is necessary also to understand. From every part of the world comes the demand for books that will help the Christian to understand his faith, to find the answers to the questions that he and other men are asking, and to know how to present the Faith to others. The series *World Christian Books* is planned to help in this particular area of Christian need. The books are directed in the first place to the " younger Churches ", but the old distinction between younger and older Churches no longer really holds. All Churches are faced by the same problems. In all countries the same questions are being asked. The series is specially planned for those who are called to preach and teach, in the hope that the materials given in these books may help them to carry out their task more effectively. But the aim has also been to write so simply that ordinary members of the Church who wish to study their Faith may be able to use these books as individuals or in study groups and so to grow in knowledge and understanding.

The books are being published first in English, but it is intended that as soon as possible they should be made available in the main languages of the Christian world. Writers have been chosen from various countries and various branches of the Church, with special emphasis on the younger Churches. This means that there will be a variety of voices, but the aim and the hope is that through many minds and many tongues the faith of the Church in its one Lord may be clearly set forth.

STEPHEN NEILL,
Bishop.

CONTENTS

CHAPTER ONE

ON BEING A CHRISTIAN

To be a Christian means to be like Jesus Christ. There are many other ways of expressing what it means to be a Christian; but every one of them leads up to this truth—that the Christian must daily grow more like Jesus Christ. When Jesus called His first disciples, He said to them simply " Follow me ". They were to be with Him, to hear His words, to watch what He did, to learn of Him, and so to grow to be like Him. Without all this, they could not become *apostles*; for one who wishes truly to proclaim Christ must not merely speak about Him, but must also bring Him visibly before the eyes of the hearer. We shall never be perfectly like Christ; as we try to follow Him, He seems to be very far ahead of us in the way; but " Follow me " is still the rule for us, as it was for the first disciples.

Even those who are not Christians know that Christians ought to be like Christ. A great many people, even in a non-Christian country, have a very good idea of what Jesus was like; they know at least that He was just and gentle and pure and true. It may well happen to a Christian to be told his faults by one who is not a Christian : " You are a Christian; you have no business to tell lies like that. Jesus Christ would not have got angry, as you are angry," and so on. The word " Christ-like " is quite well-known and understood. A missionary once even overheard one non-Christian say to another : " That was not very Christ-like of you."

It is never pleasant to be told our faults. Often, when others point out our failures, we are inclined to say " Of course, we are poor weak creatures. Do not look at us; look at Christ, and you will see what you ought to be." To this there is a simple and perfect answer: " We cannot see Jesus Christ, but we can see you. You tell us that Jesus can save men from their sins. But are we better or easier to save than you? If Jesus has done such a bad job of saving you, why should we think that He will make a better job of saving us? "

We ought to be able to say " Look at us ". It would be wise on our part never to say anything of the kind aloud, since that would seem like pride, and to the Christian pride is one of the worst of sins. But we ought to be able humbly to hope that, when others look at us, they will see in us something of Christ. It is in this spirit that Paul does write to his friends: " Be imitators of me, as I am of Christ " (1 Cor. 11 : 1). What he meant was something like this: " I keep my eyes fixed on Christ, and try to do what I see Him do; keep your eyes fixed on me, and make what I do the pattern for your own actions." This is not empty pride on Paul's part. He has been a Christian longer than those to whom he writes, and knows more of what it means to be a Christian. So he offers himself as a guide to his friends, as they too try to grow more like Christ.

In the New Testament the growing likeness of the Christian to Christ is expressed in various ways, and often in terms of " being made new ", or " being changed ". In Colossians 3 : 9–10, we read " You have put off the old nature with its practices and have put on the new nature, which is being *renewed* in knowledge after the image of its creator ". In the beginning man was created in the image of God (Gen. 1 : 27); through Christ we are being brought back to what it was always

10

the will of God that we should be. In Romans 12 : 2, we find together the ideas of *newness* and of *change*: " Be transformed by the renewal of your mind." Here the word " transformed " is the same as that used of the Transfiguration of Jesus, when " the appearance of his countenance was altered, and his raiment became dazzling white " (Luke 9 : 29). The same idea is found again in 2 Cor. 3 : 18: " We all . . . are being changed into his likeness from one degree of glory to another; for this comes from the Lord who is the Spirit." Here is added the new thought that it is through the Holy Spirit that this transformation is to be brought about.

These verses give us the picture of what ought to happen, and also set us our problem. We know that we ought to be like Christ; we know that we are not like Christ. Is any change possible? If so, how can it be brought about?

First let us rule out two methods, which, if we follow them, will only end in disappointment.

One of the most famous Christian books ever written is called *The Imitation of Christ* (15th century A.D.). Now this book does not tell us to imitate Christ in the sense of copying Him. If it did, it would not help us in our Christian purpose. Some preachers try to copy a famous preacher, even to the details of his manner and of the way in which he expresses himself. They always end by being bad preachers. They cannot *be* the other man; and in trying to be him, they cease to be themselves. It is not in this way that we are to become like Jesus. It is a good thing that the Gospels give us so few personal details about Him. We do not know whether He was tall or short, or anything else about His physical form. This guards us against trying to be like Him through copying Him in outward things. The change we need

11

could never come in that way: it can come only through some power that works from within.

Secondly, we cannot become like Jesus through rules and laws. There must be some rules for the life of the Christian and of the Church; but they ought to be very few. The Jews tried to have a rule for everything, and Saul of Tarsus tried to keep all the rules. At the end of it, he found that it was no use; even when he had kept all the rules, his heart was not right with God, and so he had no peace. Laws and rules can never express the true meaning of Christian faith. St. Augustine in the fourth century was very near the truth when he wrote " Love, and do what you like ." The man who really loves God and his neighbour is the free man; he does not need rules, because the power of love in his heart will keep him from doing anything that will injure others, or anything that will bring dishonour to the name of God.

The needed change can come only through a power working from within; " this comes from the Lord who is the Spirit " (2 Cor. 3 : 18).

In the New Testament the Holy Spirit is the Spirit of Jesus, and is so called, e.g. in Acts 16 : 7 " the Spirit of Jesus did not allow them ". It is sometimes difficult to see any difference between what is said of the risen Christ dwelling in our hearts by faith (Eph. 3 : 17), and of the Holy Spirit dwelling in us (Rom. 8 : 11). But we can note one difference. We are never told to be *like* the Spirit. We *are* told that we are to be changed into the likeness of Christ.

The Spirit is *the active force*, at work with us and within us. Sometimes the work of the Spirit has been seen in unusual, even violent, forms, such as the gift of speaking in strange tongues. The early Christians were in danger of thinking that these gifts or activities were specially important. St. Paul has to point out to them that this is not so, and that the most important work of the Spirit is to be seen in the transformation of character (1 Cor. 12 : 2–14: 40; especially 12 : 31–13 : 2).

Jesus Christ, as He is shown to us in the Gospels, is, we may say, *the standard* by which the change in us is to be judged. St. Paul teaches us that the first fruit of the Spirit is love. We learn what love is from studying in the Gospel the love that Jesus had for His friends (John 15 : 13). If we see in a single Christian or in a Christian group an increase of that kind of love, we may feel sure that the Spirit of Jesus is at work. If we do not see such love in a group which claims to be specially filled with the Spirit, we may well be doubtful as to whether their claim is true or not.

The Holy Spirit is the source of all our goodness. But God always treats us as *persons*. That is to say, He does not merely do things to us. He waits until we are willing to let Him work and to work with Him, or at least to prepare the way for His coming.

What, then, can we do to prepare the way for the coming of the Holy Spirit, and to help Him in His work?

1. The start must be our careful reading of the Gospels. What was Jesus really like? We shall never be able to find a final answer to this question. The character of Jesus is like a deep clear pool; we may think that, if we reach our hand down into the water, we shall be able to touch the bottom; yet the further we stretch, the further the bottom seems to be from us. But, if we study the Gospels patiently, we shall come to know Jesus better; and to know Him better is the first step towards growing more like Him.

2. The second step is to learn to look towards Jesus at all times: " looking to Jesus the pioneer and perfecter of our faith " (Heb. 12 : 2). It is a good thing

to know Jesus as He was long ago in Galilee and Judaea, but that is not enough. We need to know Him as a living Friend to-day. Some people have a greater gift than others for being still, and feeling the presence of the living Christ. Most of us find this very difficult. Yet everyone can learn something of it. To begin with, it is quite enough to sit still for two minutes, and to keep on bringing our minds and our thoughts back to the living Christ. It is surprising how many times our thoughts can wander away even in two minutes; but they can always be brought back to the living Christ, and to His unfailing love for us.

3. The third step is to think seriously about our work and our friends and our problems, as God thinks about them. Can a man really think as God thinks? Never perfectly: God's thoughts are always higher than our thoughts (Isa. 55 : 9); but we know from the Bible a great deal about the way in which God thinks, and St. Paul tells us that " We have the mind of Christ " (1 Cor. 2 : 16). If we try to think as God thinks, we shall find over and over again that something within us says " You must do this ", " You cannot do that ". Why? Is there a rule against it? " No; but love forbids, and you know that God has something better for you to do than that."

4. Most important of all is not to resist the Holy Spirit. A great Christian teacher once said that the real problem is " I can be good if I want to; but I don't want to." We know that we ought to say " Yes ", but something inside us says " No ". When we do wrong, we speak of the strength of the temptation and so on; but often we do not admit that the enemy outside the gates had a friend inside the gates—that part of us which says " No " when it ought to say " Yes ", and " Yes " when it ought to say " No ". We cannot ourselves deal

14

with this enemy inside the gates; he is part of ourselves and we cannot get rid of him. But, if we are not willing to admit that he is there, we make it easy for him to overcome that part of us which wants to do God's will. The Holy Spirit cannot help us, unless we are honest, and admit how much we need His help. To refuse to admit our need of help is to resist the Holy Spirit.

We do not grow into likeness to Christ by obeying a number of rules. What we are concerned with is the formation of a character. A character is formed by many hundreds, many thousands, of decisions. We have to choose and to decide many times every day. There are very few decisions which can exactly be covered by any rule; naturally, because laws are fixed and dead, and life, just because it is alive, is always changing and in movement.

It is useful, however, to have some *principles*, which may help to guide us in our decisions. The New Testament does not simply tell us to be like Christ; it does help to show us in some detail what we are to try to do. St. Paul tells his friends that they are not under law but under grace. But several times he gives them lists of the bad deeds that they are to avoid, and the good qualities at which they are to aim (e.g. Col. 3 : 5–4 : 6). The best known of these lists is that given in Galatians 5 : 22–23; after a long list of the evils that appear in human nature, Paul gives a picture of the character that will be seen in those who are transformed by the Holy Spirit: " The fruit of the Spirit is love, joy, peace, patience, kindness, goodness, faithfulness, gentleness, self-control." This is not meant to be a complete list of all the possible Christian virtues; it tells us the *kind* of people that we ought to be. In fact this may be taken as a brief sketch of what Jesus Christ was like. At the end of our study, which will be based on these nine virtues, the reader might well go back to the Gospels, and see how each of these virtues is to be seen in the life and actions of Jesus. A famous Christian teacher wrote that " the fruits of the Spirit are simply the virtues of Christ ".

These nine qualities fall roughly into three groups, corresponding, but in the opposite order, to the three words, " soberly and righteously and godly " (R.V.) in Titus 2 : 12:

in relation to God:	love, joy, peace;
in relation to other men:	patience, kindness, goodness;
in relation to ourselves:	faithfulness, gentleness, self-control.

It is important to note that St. Paul speaks of these nine virtues as " the *fruit* of the Spirit ". The Spirit is one, and I am one. I am called to be obedient to God in all things. If by His help I am obedient to Him in one respect, I shall become in all things more like Christ, and in all respects my character will begin to show that likeness.

In some books on the Christian life the reader is advised to aim at one virtue at a time. This year make it your aim to be more gentle; next year go on and make it your aim to be more humble, and so on. Sometimes the advice is given in the other way—that we should try to free ourselves from one vice at a time: this year try to overcome anger; then next year go on to overcome pride. Experience shows that this method just does not work.

The fruit of the Spirit is one, and the work of evil is one. All virtues come from one root, and all vices come from one root. The root of all virtue is to abide in Christ. The root of all vice is to be out of Christ. The man who

16

abides in Christ brings forth good fruit as naturally as the branch which abides in the vine: " Abide in me, and I in you. . . . He who abides in me, and I in him, he it is that bears much fruit, for apart from me you can do nothing " (John 15 : 4, 5). If at any moment we have done wrong, it was because we were not abiding in Christ. When we abide in Christ, we are safe, even when temptation is strong and fierce.

Every virtue is a form of obedience to God. Every evil word or act is a form of rebellion against Him. This may not be clear at first; but, if we think patiently, we shall find that it is true. Why were you angry? You will probably find that it was because you were not willing to accept the world as God has made it; or because you were not willing to leave it to God to deal with the people that He has made.

All of us have been rebels against God. Something of that rebellion remains in all of us. But it shows itself in different ways in each of us. Some folk are very hard-working and honest in their work, but very easily get angry; others are patient and do not lose their temper, but are careless in their work. The nine virtues which we are to study are like a mirror held up in front of us, in order that we may know ourselves. If we make the study carefully, we shall be able to see in which of the virtues we are weakest, and into which of the vices we most easily fall.

The next step is to try to find out where rebellion against God still hides itself in our heart. It may hide itself in any one of many forms. One of the commonest is simply that we are not willing to accept as friends those with whom God has set us to live. When we have found the heart of the problem, there are three steps to be taken:

1. To remind ourselves that our business is to obey

God in all things, and not just in the things in which we like to obey Him.

2. To look long and quietly to Christ in order to see how He dealt with the problem we have to face.

3. To open our hearts to the Holy Spirit, in order that willing obedience to God in all things may come to us as His gift and through His power.

Evidently, learning to be like Christ is going to demand of us much attention and much hard work—but not quite the kind of hard work that most people imagine. The hard work of serving Christ in the world will become easy, if we have first done the harder work that has to be done inside ourselves. This is the " fight of faith ". It means learning not to be restless and in a hurry, but to be willing to be still and to wait until we can *hear* the Spirit speak. It means learning not to say " *I* must overcome this or that failing ", but to be willing to *receive* from the Holy Spirit grace to do what we cannot achieve ourselves. It means learning not to say " *I* will do this or that ", but to *surrender* ourselves more fully to God, that His will may be done in and through us.

Those who try to follow Christ are often sad because they seem to make so little progress. But, if they are really looking to Christ, they have no need to worry about themselves. It is good that so often we do not know about our own progress. If we knew, we might become proud, and it is much safer to be humble. But others will certainly see the progress that we have made; they will understand something of the work of Christ in us, and " recognize that we have been with Jesus " (Acts 4 : 13).

CHAPTER TWO

LOVE

" Thou shalt love thy neighbour as thyself." This is the second great commandment. But can we really be ordered to love someone? Is not love something that just comes of itself? If we are told to love someone, is not the result likely to be just the opposite—that we dislike that person we have been told to love? " Who ever loved that loved not at first sight? " asks the poet. We do not look for love; it just comes. We do not know why we choose our friends; we like some people and not others, and often we find it very difficult to say why. How then can " love thy neighbour " be directed to us as a command?

The Bible does not deny this natural human love. It is full of lovely pictures of it—of the love of Jacob for Rachel, of Ruth for her mother-in-law, of David for Jonathan his friend, of Jesus for His disciples. This human affection, by which we are drawn to one another, is still the strongest power in the world; the love of husband and wife, of parents for their children, of friend for friend is the source of most of the happiness in our lives. But what the Bible tells us is that this is not enough. We have to learn to extend to *all* men that which we find natural in relation to *some*; we have to learn to exercise *love*, even when we are not moved by the inner feeling of *affection*.

Let us make no mistake. " Love thy neighbour " is

not good advice: " It would be nice if everyone loved everyone else." It is a command; and in the Bible, if commands are given, it is because they are expected to be obeyed.

One of the greatest books on this subject is *The Works of Love*, which was written by the great Danish thinker Søren Kierkegaard in 1847. The first three chapters of the book are called " Thou *shalt* love "; " Thou shalt love *thy neighbour* "; " *Thou* shalt love thy neighbour ".

" Thou *shalt* love." Many wonderful things have been written by the poets about love; but nearly always they have been writing about emotion and passion and desire. The new truth that is shown in the Gospel is that love is made a duty: " Only when it is a duty to love, only then is love for ever safe against every change, for ever set free in blessed independence; for ever happy, assured against despair."

" Thou shalt love *thy neighbour*." Our friends are the people whom we choose; usually friends are the same sort of people as ourselves. My neighbour is the man whom I do not choose; he is the man whom God gives to me. He is the man who happens to live in the house next to mine; he is the man who happens to sit opposite to me in the train; he is the clerk who works at the desk next to mine. I have no right to say that he is no concern of mine, because, if I am a Christian, I know that he is the man whom *God* has given to *me*.

" *Thou* shalt love thy neighbour." This is not a general command, given to the whole human race. It is not a word to specially good people, or to those who have a natural sympathy for others. It is a direct word of God to *me*, here and now, where I am. It is addressed to *me*, whether I like it or not. It is not a command which I may push away into the future, to be thought about when I have more time. It is a word spoken to *me* by God *to-day*. Who is my neighbour to-day? Am I prepared to obey the command that I am to love him?

We must first make it clear that there are two quite different kinds of love, which in most languages are referred to by the same word.

The first love says " I wish to make my own something that another has, and which it is in his power to give me."

The second love says " I wish to give to this other, because I love him."

The first love wishes to make itself richer by receiving a gift which some other can give.

The second love wishes to make another richer by giving all that it has.

The first love is a matter of feeling and desire. This love comes and goes as it will; we cannot call it into being by any effort of our own.

The second love is much more a matter of the will, since to give or not to give is largely within our power. Of course, feeling is always a part of love; but in this kind of love, the feeling of affection for a person often comes *after* the resolution to serve him has been taken, and not *before*. In this sense, we can say " I *will* love ".

We can see both kinds of love at work in marriage. In one marriage, each desires to *get* something from the other—physical pleasure, support, help, service. These two will make one another poorer all the time, and by the end of six months they may well be utterly weary of one another. In another case, each wishes only to give to the other everything that he or she has, without asking anything in return. Such a pair can live together happily for fifty years, since each is growing richer all the time by what the other is gladly giving. By asking nothing, each gains far more than could be gained by asking; and yet the purpose of each is only to give and not to gain.

Love in the Bible sense of the word is always concerned with *self-giving*. It is never merely feeling; it always includes " a steady direction of the will towards another's lasting good ".

This will become clear, if we think of the nature of God's love for us. Because He is love, His loving will is only for the good of all men everywhere. Because He is God, He never changes. His *action* may change, since He is always free to do what is right; and, in this changing world, what is right at one time may not be right at another. But His *will* is always the same, and it is always for our good. This explains how it is possible for God to love sinners, even while they are sinners, and before they turn to Him. He loves us not because we are good, but because of His own will and purpose to lead us to goodness.

We cannot always see this to be true; but when we look back over the past it may become clearer. God sometimes leads us through very dark ways, and in times of pain or sorrow we find ourselves tempted to think that He has forgotten us, or even that He hates us. Later we may come to understand that what seemed like harm was really a source of good, and that His loving hand was over us even in the valley of the shadow of death. " In everything God works for good with those who love him " (Rom. 8 : 28) is perhaps the hardest verse in the Bible to believe; but those who are willing to trust God do find in the end that it is true.

The same definition will teach us how we are to love those by whom we are surrounded. Love is an activity in which the will has a vital part to play. Feelings will certainly come and go; with the help of God, the will can remain firm. Love demands a " steady direction of the will ". This means that we have to accept people as people, with a whole life to live, as we live ours. We must not take an interest in them just for a moment and then let it drop. Our interest must be in their life and their needs as a whole. And the will must be directed to the other's lasting good. We cannot always give people just what they want. To give a beggar money may seem kind (and sometimes is the right thing to do), but it may be the very worst thing that we could do for him. No wise parent always gives a child what it wants; the result of doing so is too well known. Spoilt children are always terrible; and it is very difficult to correct in later life the faults that they have learned when young.

It is possible and sometimes necessary for love to be very stern. If we really love another person, we wish that person to be as good as he can possibly be. If we see him going in the wrong way, we are sad and angry, not because we hate him but because we love him, and cannot bear to see him being less of a man than he ought to be. The world is a hard place; it is no kindness to a child to bring it up to believe that it is a soft and easy one. In any good home there is an element of sternness and discipline; and no sensible child thinks that there is any contradiction between the love by which it is guarded, and the sternness through which it learns to obey.

We can now understand the meaning of the command to love our enemy. Here both words must be taken in their full sense. Your enemy is the man who is out to harm you, perhaps even to take away your life. To love him does not mean simply to do him less harm than he has done you; it means, if necessary, to be willing to give your own life in order to do him good.

We are not told to like our enemy, to have that warm kindly feeling towards him which we have towards our friend; we are told to set our wills to do him all the good that is in our power. That does not always mean making things easy for him. We are called to forgive from the heart every injury that he has done to us, and to do everything that we can to bring him back to a better way. But the way back is not always easy. Sometimes, for the sake of others, and for the sake of society, it is the duty of Christians to work with the human justice of the state, not out of anger or hatred, but because in the end this may be the best thing also for the one who has done the wrong. Does our description of love cover also the love that we ought to show to God? Clearly the words will not mean quite the same as when we speak of our love for other men; but still they can be used. A wise teacher, in explaining the Lord's Prayer, headed one section of his explanation " Praying for God "! When we pray " Thy kingdom come; thy will be done on earth ", what are we doing, except helping God by our prayers to do something that He wishes to do, but will not do without our help? How do we know that we love God? We must learn not to depend on the warm pleasant feelings that sometimes, but not always, come when we pray or when we think about God. Love to God is shown, and is known, in obeying His orders (1 John 5 : 3). In fact we learn to love God by setting our wills steadfastly to do His will; if we do so, it will not be long before we experience the wonderful enrichment of every part of our being that comes to those who truly love God.

If love includes an attitude of the will, it is certain that love will soon show itself in action.

The Bible tells us that this is true of God. He is loving towards men: His love is seen in what He did.

This is true in the Old Testament. Here is a beautiful picture of the love of God, as Israel had come to know it: " In his love and in his pity he redeemed them; he lifted them up and carried them all the days of old " (Isaiah 63 : 9). The same truth is set forth even more clearly in the New Testament: " God so loved the world that he gave his only Son " (John 3 : 16). " In this is love, not that we loved God but that he loved us and sent his Son to be the expiation for our sins " (1 John 4 : 10).

Man's love also is not true love, until it is expressed in action. When Jesus is asked " Who is my neighbour? ", he tells the story of the Good Samaritan. The *word* " love " is not used in the story, but that is what it is all about. The only thing we are told about the feelings of the Samaritan is that he had compassion on the wounded man; we are told a great deal more about what he did. He did everything that was needed, and all that was possible at the time. And to his practical first-aid to a wounded man he added the kind thought that a man who has been robbed of all his money will need some money to keep him going (Luke 10 : 29–37).

My neighbour is any man who is in need and whom I might help. When Jesus taught this, it was new doctrine. The old idea may be described as that of putting a man in the centre, and drawing a series of circles round him; first he must love those of his own family; then those of his own city and tribe; then he may spare a little for strangers and foreigners; and finally perhaps he may even find it possible to love his enemy. Jesus says, on the contrary, that at any moment any man may become the one to whom you must show yourself as neighbour. Your love is not a general kindly feeling towards all men. It is obedience, which is ready to run to the help of each particular man, when God

25

brings him near you and puts you in the position where you might help him.

The Church has a great record of serving those who are in need. But also very often it has been blind. On the whole the great movements which have benefited mankind have not arisen from the action of the Church as a whole; much more generally they began with one man being faced with one particular need, and saying " What can I do to meet this one need? " In the eighteenth century Granville Sharp was faced by the need of one African brought to England as a slave. He fought the case of that one man in the law courts, until the decision was given which made it impossible for any man ever again to be a slave in England. We are not told whether Granville Sharp had strong feelings of personal affection for the African concerned. But, by spending time and strength and health and money on the case, he showed what real Christian love can be.

The greatest gift that any man can give to any other is Christ. Very few people pass even a single day without being in touch with someone who does not know Christ, and who greatly needs to know Him. Can we pretend that we love, if we are not passing on the knowledge of Him?

Is not all this very difficult? This doctrine of love seems to make great demands on me. Can I meet them? Let us recall that this love which we are studying is described as a fruit of the Spirit; not something that we can work up ourselves, but something which God is willing to give us as a gift. *How* does the Holy Spirit produce this love in us? To that question, fortunately, the answer is not doubtful. It is set out very plainly in the New Testament: "We love, because he first loved us" (1 John 4: 19, R.S.V. Note that this, and not the A.V.

" We love him ", is the correct translation). How does a child learn what love is? Through being loved by its parents; it knows by experience what love is, long before it knows the word. How do we know what love is? Because God has loved us. " By this we know love, that he laid down his life for us; and we ought to lay down our lives for the brethren " (1 John 3 : 16).

If you feel that you do not love as you should, let the Holy Spirit lead you back to Gethsemane and Calvary. If, through the Holy Spirit's help, you really see and feel the love of God for you, as shown in the death of Jesus Christ for you, it is certain that through gratitude an answer of love will be heard in your heart. Because He loved and gave for you, you will want to love and give to Him. But how can you better give to Him than by helping His children who are in need of your help? He will open your eyes to see those who are in need of help. And when you show your love by helping and serving them, you will no longer need to ask whether you love God or no.

The New Testament tells us, not only that God loves, but that God is love. When we love, we touch the most eternal thing that exists. St. Paul shows us why this is so: " So faith, hope, love abide, these three; but the greatest of these is love " (1 Cor. 13 : 13). On earth we trust God, whom here on earth we cannot see. But in heaven there will be no need for faith, since we shall see God as He is. Here we hope for that which has not yet been given, and patiently wait for it. In heaven all hopes will have been fulfilled, and so there will be nothing left to hope for. But love will go on for ever. We try to love God even here, though we know that we can never love Him as we would wish to do. There we shall see and know just how much He has loved us. That knowledge will set us free to love Him as we can never love Him on earth. We shall love Him as we ought, because we shall see Him as He is. And we shall see all His other children in Him. Here our best love of others is poor and weak, often faint and often unwise. Love always brings joy. No small part of the joy of heaven will consist in being able to love others perfectly, and in knowing that we are perfectly loved by them. Eternity can bring no end to the increase of love, and to the joy of God's children in loving and being loved.

CHAPTER THREE

JOY

It was because they were a joyful people that the early Christians were able to conquer the world.

The world into which they came, like our world to-day, was not a very happy world.

In earlier days the Greeks had had a deep, spontaneous joy in life. They loved beauty, and they created beauty in wonderful poems and buildings and statues. The Romans had had immense vigour, and through it had won a great empire. But that old world was growing tired. After many wars the Roman emperors had brought peace to men. But with peace life had grown dull, and men were beginning to wonder what there was to live for. There was little idea of progress. The common idea was that history goes round in a great circle; after many years, all things come back exactly to what they were before, and then the same old story starts all over again. Very few had hope of a better life after death. Many thousands of inscriptions from ancient tombs have been collected. Almost all speak of sorrow; hardly a single one speaks of hope.

Upon this grey world the Christians burst with their tidings of great joy. The New Testament speaks of joy in at least a hundred and fifty places. Joy was one of the marks by which Christians were known; St. Peter explains the nature of this unfailing and triumphant joy:
" You believe in him and rejoice with unutterable and

exalted joy. As the outcome of your faith you obtain the salvation of your souls " (1 Peter 1 : 8–9).

There are three Greek words for joy in the New Testament.

The first is used of the cheerfulness natural to us in the society of our friends; the father of the prodigal son says that it was right *to make merry*, because the son who was dead has come back to life (Luke 15 : 32).

The second word speaks of the joy that is a gift of God. " The kingdom of God . . . [is] righteousness and peace and joy in the Holy Spirit " (Romans 14 : 17).

The third adds the idea of the outward signs by which joy is known; it can almost be translated " shout for joy ". In a moment of special emotion, Jesus " rejoiced in the Holy Spirit " (Luke 10 : 21); He cried out for joy in some of the most wonderful words that even He ever spoke.

The joy of the Christians looked backward to the past and forward to the future, and gave them calm courage in the present.

The starting point was the resurrection of Jesus Christ. " Then the disciples were glad when they saw the Lord " (John 20 : 20). They knew that the great event of history had happened. The great victory had already been won. God had shown that love is stronger than hate, and that life is stronger than death. Who can be sad in a world in which Jesus has risen from the dead?

The Christians rejoiced in hope (Romans 12 : 12, and see Romans 5 : 2). They knew that one day history would come to an end, and that God's kingdom of love alone would remain. The seer of the Revelation heard great voices saying " Hallelujah! For the Lord our God the Almighty reigns. Let us rejoice and exult " (Rev.

19 : 6, 7). Christians knew that they would have a share in that joy. So even death had no terrors for them. St. Paul, thinking of his own death, speaks of it as " to depart and be with Christ, for that is far better " (Phil. 1 : 23). To the Christian, to die is simply to be with Christ; and where Christ is, there is joy.

Jesus had promised that He would always be with His disciples, and had told them that " no one will take your joy from you " (John 16 : 22). They found that it was true; because the Lord was with them, no suffering or hardship could take away their joy. When the Apostles were first called to suffer, and were beaten by the Jews, they went out " rejoicing that they were counted worthy to suffer dishonour for the Name " (Acts 5 : 41). The Epistle to the Philippians was written when St. Paul was in prison, never knowing when he might be called to suffer death for Christ's sake. Yet no book in the New Testament speaks so much about joy. " Rejoice in the Lord always; again I will say, Rejoice " is the message of the Apostle (Phil. 4 : 4).

Joy is not very much in evidence in the world to-day. Poverty and hunger are still the lot of the majority. Even in the prosperous countries riches do not seem to have brought happiness with them. After two world wars, men's hearts easily fail them for fear of what may be coming on the earth. Many have lost the hope of life after death, and do not really know what they are living for. Such a world needs the message of joy just as much as the world into which Jesus was born; to-day, as in the days of the Apostles, Christians ought to be known by the joy which no man can take from them.

" Rejoice always, pray constantly " (1 Thess. 5 : 16–17). St. Paul gives these two commands together; and we find each of them about as difficult to fulfil as the other. We can be happy sometimes. But is it really possible to be joyful all the time, no matter what troubles or sorrow may have come upon us? Certainly this is not easy. But the joy of which we are speaking is called a fruit of the Spirit; it is He who can give us a joy that never fails.

It would be convenient if we could clearly distinguish between pleasure, happiness and joy. Most languages have these three words; but unfortunately they are not kept clearly separate, and one word is often used in the sense which belongs to another. Even in the New Testament we cannot say that the three ideas are kept quite distinct from one another. What are these three ideas?

We may use the word " pleasure " of that which comes to us *from* things, and *through* our senses. Some Christians have held the view that all pleasure was bad in itself. This is false. Certainly some pleasures are evil, and others dangerous. But the New Testament teaches us that God " richly furnishes us with everything to enjoy " (1 Tim. 6 : 17). Yet the nature of pleasure is that at any moment it can be taken from us. One man takes special pleasure in looking at beautiful pictures. If he goes blind, he will never see another picture. One man loves listening to beautiful music. He may go deaf, and then, though he may remember music from the past, he will never hear music again. We have the right to enjoy every good thing that God gives us; but we must not set our hearts too much on these things, remembering that they can be taken away from us.

Happiness we may regard as that which comes *from* people and *through* fellowship. This is higher than pleasure. Pleasure can be very selfish. Real happiness can come only when we give ourselves to others, and receive them, as they give themselves to us. God has set men to live in families; it is His will that the love of husband and wife and children should be one of our chief sources of happiness. But, like pleasure, happiness can be taken away from us. Most of us have had at some time to share the sorrow of those who have grieved over the loss of an only son. Most of us know people who seem to have lost all those whom they have loved and to be alone in the world. Such people often bear their loss with great courage. But we know, and they know, that happiness such as they have had in the past can never come to them again.

Now joy, in the sense in which Jesus uses the word, is something that can never be taken from us. Pleasure can fail; happiness can be taken away. Where then is joy to be found? The answer is clear. It is only to be found in and through Him who Himself never changes. The message of St. Paul to his friends is not simply " Rejoice ". It is " Rejoice in the Lord ". The joy that He gives dwells so deep in our hearts that nothing can touch or harm it. Jesus Christ is the same yesterday, to-day and for ever (Heb. 13 : 8). All earthly things may change; but since He does not change, the joy that He gives remains with us for ever.

This was the joy of Jesus Christ. It was on the last night of His life, when His enemies were all around Him, that He spoke to His disciples of the joy that no man taketh away (John 16 : 23 and see also Heb. 12 : 2). Read again the story of the passion. Jesus is seen throughout as calm, quiet and confident. His last word is " Father, into thy hands I commit my spirit " (Luke 23 : 46). Someone may say " Yes, but He knew that He was going to rise from the dead." But have we not the same promise for ourselves?

The ordinary group of worshipping Christians, as the preacher sees them from the pulpit, does not look like a collection of very joyful people; in fact, they look on the whole rather sad, tired, depressed people. It is certain that such people will never win the world for Christ. But sometimes also the preacher does not look very much like a man who is bringing good news. If this is true, the situation is serious. It is no use trying to pretend. We may speak of joy and preach about it. But, unless we really have the joy of Christ in our hearts and manifest it, our words will carry no conviction to our hearers, whether Christian or non-Christian.

But can we really rejoice, when there is so much to make us unhappy?

Let us turn back to the New Testament. St. Paul's words " Rejoice in the Lord always " are a command—a command that we are expected to obey. We are not allowed to say " I will rejoice, when the feeling of joy comes to me ", as it does to all of us from time to time; or, " when life becomes a little easier for me, I shall be able to rejoice ". No; here and now. If God gives a command, He will give also the grace to fulfil it.

Let us think of some of the things over which, even in dark times, we ought to be able to rejoice:

1. God has made the world full of beautiful things, and has given it to us to enjoy.

2. Jesus Christ really has died for our sins, and set us free from all the powers of evil.

3. Jesus Christ really has risen from the dead, and given us a share in His resurrection.

4. Jesus Christ really is with us all the time, as the Son of God was with the three young men who were thrown into the burning fiery furnace.

5. God has promised to work with us for good in all things, and to turn even troubles and sorrows into a source of joy.

6. God really does rule the world, and is leading all things forward to the triumph of His cause.

7. God has given us work to do, and depends on our faithfulness.

8. When we feel that we are alone, we are still part of an immense fellowship of Christian people in paradise and all over the world.

9. When we die, we are simply going to be with Jesus, which is very far better.

10. God has promised to us a place in His heavenly kingdom, where joy will be made perfect in His presence.

Can anyone really read through this list, stopping to think for a moment of each point in it, and continue to be sad and forlorn? If we continue to be sad, it is only because we have not dug deep enough to find the joy which God has ready for us just in the place where we are.

Some years ago the Christians of a village in India came to me and said " Our well is already dry, and there is no hope of rain for four months. What shall we do? " I said, " I think there is water deeper down; try boring a shaft in the middle of your well." For six days they worked, and nothing came. The seventh, they came to me radiant with joy and said, " There is water in the well to the height of two men! " They had pierced the hard rock, and forty feet down they had found the hidden stream. Since that day the well has never gone dry. In the hottest weather, when everything all round is scorched and dry, it is always surrounded by a brilliant strip of green. The water was there all the time. When they went deep enough, they found it, and then their hearts were filled with joy.

CHAPTER FOUR

PEACE

What is peace? Probably most people would answer that it is the state of things which comes about when there is no war. When war ends, peace begins.

Of course that is quite true. The Greek word in the New Testament which is translated " peace " does mean in the old Greek authors " the state of affairs when there is no war ". But, if we look at the Old Testament, we shall find a rather different and a richer meaning. The Hebrew word *Shalom*[1] comes from a root which means " fulness, perfection ". In the beautiful promise in Isaiah 26 : 3 " Thou dost keep him in perfect peace, whose mind is stayed on thee ", " perfect peace " in the Hebrew is just the word " peace " twice repeated. If we take account of this root-meaning of the word, we shall find that peace, in the Bible sense of the word, may be defined as " the state of things which comes about, when God's will is being done ". In many places, we could almost translate *Shalom* by the word " salvation ". " I know the thoughts that I think toward you, saith the Lord, thoughts of peace. and not of evil " (Jer. 29 : 11, R.V.) Even though His people are captives in a far off land, God will in the end bring them back safely to their own land. Then " great shall be the peace of thy children ".

[1] This is the same as the Arabic *salaam*, so widely used as a greeting in many lands of Africa and the East.

This means much more than just that they shall be free from the fear of their enemies; since then: " All thy children shall be taught of the Lord " (Isa. 54 : 13, R.V.).

Peace is that state of things which exists when God's will is being done. But sin has entered into the world, and God's will is not being done. And where God's will is not being done, there strife is found. Man is born to be the child of God, but he has become the enemy of God. Man is at war with himself. He knows what is good and what is bad. Yet often, even when he longs to do what is right, he finds that instead he does the evil which he hates.

The message of the Gospel is that God has taken action in this world of disorder, to bring it back to its true and normal state. " God is not a God of confusion but of peace " (1 Cor. 14 : 33). So, when Jesus is born into the world, the first message of the angels is " On earth peace among men with whom he is pleased " (Luke 2 : 14). He is the One in whom the will of God will perfectly be done; through Him the world will be brought back to the way of peace from which it has strayed. Later, when the disciples were sent out to preach, they were told to say on entering into a house " Peace to this house ". This was not meant simply as a polite greeting; it was a gift offered to those in the house: " Salvation is now in the world, because God is at work in a new way through Christ. Receive this gift, if you will." If there was a son of peace in the house, that is, one who was able to understand what gift it was that was being offered, he would receive it with joy; but if not, the gift, the peace, must be taken back, because there was no one to receive it (Luke 10 : 5–6; cp. Matt. 10 : 13).

What is the position of Christians in the world? They

have received peace as a gift from God. This peace must be passed on to all the world. But most men are not ready to receive the peace of God. Therefore the preaching of the good news of peace is itself often the cause of strife. Jesus Himself foresaw this. The most terrible of all His words is this: " Do not think that I have come to bring peace on earth; I have not come to bring peace, but a sword " (Matt. 10 : 34). The Christian is always caught between the peace of Jesus and the sword of Jesus.

It has been well said that St. Paul's view of life can be summed up in the words:

> " No peace, except I struggle;
> No struggle, except I have peace."

Where shall I find peace? Many Christians have thought that they could find it by going out into the desert to seek and serve God far away from the dwellings of men. All too often they have found no peace, because they could not get away from themselves and from the war that was raging in their own hearts. Paul's answer is just the opposite to this. He must always be in the cities and among the crowds. Wherever men are with their need for God, that is where he must be. Everywhere he must take the message of Christ who " is our peace " (Eph. 2 : 14). But this is a strange way of seeking peace. In place after place, Paul finds hatred, danger and suffering—"danger in the city, danger in the wilderness, danger at sea, danger from false brethren; in toil and hardship, through many a sleepless night, in hunger and thirst, often without food, in cold and exposure" (2 Cor. 11 : 26, 27). What has all this to do with peace? Yet when Paul promises the Philippians that the peace of God shall guard their hearts and their minds (Phil 4 : 7), it is clear that he is writing of something that he has known himself.

A man cannot bear all that Paul bore, unless he has in his heart the peace that comes only as a gift from God. Of this Paul speaks to the Romans: " Therefore, since we are justified by faith, we have peace with God through our Lord Jesus Christ " (Romans 5 : 1). The next four chapters of the Epistle tell us all that this means. We were enemies to God; now we have become sons. Fear has been changed to trust. Because we are sons, we know that God's will is being done in us; and therefore, as sons, we must set to work to see that God's will is done also in the world. And that means first and foremost that the word of God's peace must be everywhere proclaimed.

The work of the Church and of the Christian to-day is exactly what it was in the days of Paul. There is a danger that people may think of the Church as a refuge for tired folk, where they may try to find peace by running away from the world. This is just the opposite of what the Church ought to be. The message of the Gospels is that God loved the world; the Church ought to be in that world which God loved and loves. The world is full of strife; it is the business of the Church to be everywhere the messenger and the bringer of peace.

First, the Church must tell the world plainly that in Jesus Christ its peace has already come. This is such good news that we might expect that the world would rejoice to hear it. But the peace of Christ cannot be received except by those who are willing to do God's will. Men as a whole prefer their own will to God's; therefore they cannot receive His peace; therefore it is likely that they will make war on those who bring the message of peace. The story of the two messengers in

Revelation 11 is a picture of the fate that may befall the Church in all times until the end of history.

But simply to proclaim the message is not enough. The Church must show what it means that the will of God is being done on earth. Wherever injustice and wrong exist, the Church must be there to say " This is not the will of God; this must be changed ". Injustice is the great cause of strife among men; wherever injustice is set right and justice is done, the cause of peace is served. In the past too often the Church has failed to bear a faithful witness. To-day we see clearly that there can be no peace upon earth, if one half of the world is slave and the other half free, if one half of the world is poor and the other half rich. Wherever men are serving the cause of justice and peace, the Church should be with them, and in the lead.

The Church is concerned also with the question of peace and war. Men have always hoped and longed for the time when there would be no more war. We cannot say when, if ever, this time will come. But to say that we cannot produce perfect peace for evermore does not set us free from the duty of earnestly seeking peace in our own day. Our history books tell us all about the wars that have happened; they do not always tell us of the wars that might have happened and did not. So many wars have been prevented, because men of goodwill sought peace at the right time and in the right way. It is the duty of Christians to pray at all times for rulers and statesmen. It should be possible for these statesmen to be sure that, if they are honestly seeking peace, they can count on the support of all Christian people in the world.

The Church, then, has a threefold duty in relation to peace on earth, peace among men—(1) to proclaim the Gospel, (2) to fight against injustice, (3) to work for fellowship among the nations. But the Church cannot fulfil this duty, unless it is at peace in itself. The saddest thing in the history of the Church is that Christians have found it so difficult to live at peace with one another.

The Church is divided, and so it is weak. Where the Spirit rules, there is peace; the Churches will find again their lost unity only when they are really ruled by the Spirit of God, and make the service of God their one and only aim.

But even in small Christian groups we often find strife, where there ought to be peace. It was so among the apostles; there was strife among them as to which should be the greatest (Luke 22 : 24). St. Paul had to appeal to two good ladies in the Church at Philippi not to quarrel (Phil. 4 : 2). Christians to-day are very much like Christians nineteen hundred years ago.

Where do these quarrels come from? Do they not arise because, like other people, Christians too often want to have their own way? We are all sure that we are right; and so perhaps, when we pray " Thy will be done ", we are really saying " My will be done; help Thou my will to prevail." Sometimes we are right; but we may insist on our views in such a way as to make other people angry. And serious quarrels among Christians can arise from such tiny causes. Even such a question as who is to sit in what seat in Church may cause a bitter quarrel lasting over many years.

We may now understand why our Lord pronounced a special blessing on the peacemakers " for they shall be called sons of God " (Matt. 5 : 9). When a serious quarrel has broken out, it is terribly hard to make peace. It is very hard for me to yield to you; my pride will not allow it. Even if I yield, outwardly, I may still have bitter feelings in my heart. How can real peace come? We already know the answer; it can come only when both sides are willing to seek the will of God and that only. Here is the task of the peacemaker. If he can get the two who have quarrelled quietly together, and help them to ask " What really is God's will? ", peace is already on the way. It may turn out, and often does, that both are wrong, and that God's will, as shown by the Holy Spirit, is something quite different from what either had thought. It may be that one is right after all. I cannot yield to you; but I can easily yield to God, if it is He who shows me that after all I was wrong. Only you must not say " You see, I was right ": we must both say " After all, God was right all the time, but one or both of us could not see it."

We are all called to be sons of God. Therefore we are all called to be peacemakers. But we cannot make peace among others, unless we have God's peace in our own hearts. In thinking of the Christian's peace, most people would put first this inner personal peace, in the sense of confidence and freedom from anxiety. In putting it last, we are following the New Testament. For in the New Testament there is very little about peace as something enjoyed by the individual. In fact, perhaps we can quote only one verse for this sense of the word peace: " May the God of hope fill you with all joy and peace in believing, so that by the power of the Holy Spirit you may abound in hope " (Rom. 15 : 13). But we do not obtain this inner peace by seeking it. We obtain it by being concerned only that God's will should be done. Jesus Christ delighted to do God's will; even in His Cross and Passion, He was free from fear and from anxiety because He knew that He was doing God's will. If we let the Spirit rule in our hearts, as He did, we shall be free from fear and from anxiety as He was. Why should we be anxious, if it is true that God in everything works for good with them that love Him? (Rom. 8 : 28). We live in a world which is full of anxiety. A Christian who lives in calm and quiet confidence in God, and makes the doing of God's will his one great concern, does stand out as different from other men around him. Other men may take note of this, and may be led to turn to the Christian, saying, " Tell us, what is the secret of your peace? "

CHAPTER FIVE

PATIENCE

There are in the Greek New Testament two words, both of which might be translated " patience ", but the meaning of which is not quite the same.

One word speaks of endurance, of standing firm in the face of difficulty or suffering without losing heart. This is the word used of the " steadfastness " of Job (James 5 : 11). Job was sorely tried by loss and suffering and sickness; yet he did not entirely give up his faith; he held on until the end.

The other word, also used in the same chapter (James 5 : 7–8), is used in relation to time; to wait until the appointed time has come, without growing impatient and angry, like the farmer waiting for his harvest; he knows that it will come in due time, and worrying over it will not make it come any quicker. It is this second word that we are to study in this chapter.

The New Testament writers have taken a familiar word and changed its meaning. In ordinary Greek this word was often a little contemptuous: " since you are human, troubles will come; you had better learn to put up with them." The English word " resignation " comes somewhere near the meaning. But the New Testament writers were able to give the word a far finer meaning, because they related it to something that they had found in the character of God Himself.

In the Old Testament, God had been revealed as "a God merciful and gracious, slow to anger, and abounding in steadfast love and faithfulness" (Ex. 34 : 6). In the Greek Old Testament, our word is used as the translation of the Hebrew "slow to anger". God is all-powerful; He could destroy the sinner at any moment. Why does He not do so? Because God is never in a hurry; He takes His time, and waits till His appointed hour has come.

Men to-day seem to be always in a hurry. But God has made a world in which things move at their own natural pace, and will not be hurried. It takes a tree fifty years to grow to its full height; if you want a tree, you must be willing to wait fifty years. Every man must pass through all the stages of childhood and boyhood before becoming a man; we do a child great harm if we try to force it to grow up more quickly than it really can.

God is not in a hurry in working out His purpose for mankind. He was prepared to take 2,000 years, from Abraham to John the Baptist, to prepare the people of Israel for the coming of His Son. There were long periods in which nothing at all seemed to be happening. There were nearly four hundred years between the Old Testament and the New. Important things were happening in history, but not one new prophet spoke until John the Baptist appeared. And still God waited; and "when the time had fully come, God sent forth his Son" (Gal. 4 : 4). It is God's purpose that the Gospel should be preached to all the world. If the Church had been obedient, surely this would have been done long ago. It is not yet done; but God seems willing to wait, and not to grow impatient when His plans are hindered by the unfaithfulness of the Church.

God waits till the harvest is ripe. It is only at the

time of harvest that the true nature of the grain can be seen. In the parable of the weeds (Matt. 13 : 24–43), the servants are in a hurry, and want to pull up the weeds; but the master is wiser, and bids them wait until the harvest, when the difference between the good grain and the bad can be easily seen. God gives men time in which to repent and turn to Him; if they refuse, the last day will make it plain that it was of their own choice that they failed to do so.

In this, as in all things, Jesus is like God. In dealing with His disciples, how patient He is! Often they are stupid and misunderstand Him; often they are unworthy of Him. But He waits; He will not reject even Judas. He gives him special privileges (John 13 : 29); He uses every possible means to win him back. But at last the true nature of Judas is seen; he is a traitor by his own free choice; nothing more can be done for him than has been already done.

We shall find that patience is a virtue of which we shall often have need ourselves, as we try to follow Christ.

First, in relation to ourselves. It takes time for our bodies to grow. It also takes time for us to grow in the life of the Spirit. We are told to " grow in grace " (2 Peter 3 : 18). Many Christians make the mistake of thinking that they can arrive at the end of their journey almost before they have begun it. Then they grow discouraged, feeling that their progress is too slow, or that they are not making any progress at all. Now in our physical life we never feel that we are growing; we only see that we have grown. It is the same in the life of the Spirit; our business is to go on quietly learning to do God's will, and giving Him time to do His work in us. There is a wonderful phrase in the Old Testament, " He that believeth shall not make haste "

(Isa. 28 : 16, R.V.). The word means that " he shall not get in a flurry of excitement ". If we try to make haste, it is certain that we shall advance much more slowly than if we are willing to have long patience, and let God work in His own way.

Second, in relation to those about us. " Be patient with them all ", writes St. Paul (1 Thess. 5 : 14). Do not get angry quickly. We must try to understand others, to give them time to show their own best and truest self. Only if we are patient can we help them when they are weak. This is specially true in the dealings of parents with children. How wise St. Paul was when he wrote " Fathers, do not provoke your children, lest they become discouraged " (Col. 3 : 21). Parents often expect their children to be wiser and better-behaved than it is natural for children to be, and so become impatient with them. But to be always finding fault may easily make the children worse instead of better! Of course this does not mean that there should be no control in the family. Children need to be guided and set in the right way. But often time and patience are the best cure for what seems to be wrong; discouragement hinders growth as much as trust and confidence encourage it.

Patience is specially needed in the work of trying to bring others to Christ. St. Paul speaks of the Galatians as " my little children, with whom I am again in travail until Christ be formed in you " (Gal. 4 : 19). A healthy child cannot be born until the long months have passed during which the child is being formed in the womb of its mother. It is very much the same with the life of the Spirit, whether we are dealing with young people who have been born within the Christian community, or with older people who are not Christian at all. Some earnest Christians try to bring young people quickly to a decision for Christ, and the results are often very disappointing. It is far better to wait longer, until the young person has learned more about Christ and has come to understand more fully what it means to accept Him as Lord. If the decision can be made gradually and quietly, but with the whole mind and will and heart, it is much more likely that it will be lasting in its effects. It is the same in dealing with non-Christians. Christian workers have often done harm by urging people to be baptized too soon. When H. A. Krishna Pillai, a young high-caste Hindu who later became a great Christian poet, was first becoming interested in the Gospel, a missionary friend said to him, " Is it not time that you were baptized ? " This was such a shock to the young man, who was not nearly ready to make such a decision, that he went right back from his first interest, and it was only after a long time that other friends were able again to interest him in the Gospel. In many cases, when converts have been baptized too soon, they have not been able to stand the strain and hardship that often follow upon baptism, and have gone back to the old ways. Time must be given for deep and strong faith to be formed in the heart. Of course, it must be made clear to people that sooner or later they must decide. We must say " Yes " or " No " to Christ; and those who cannot make up their minds to say " Yes " have in fact said " No ". But nothing is more difficult than to know at what moment to help people to make a decision. It is only the Holy Spirit who can give us the necessary wisdom both to be silent and to speak.

In work for Christ, there is often a long interval between the time of sowing and the time of reaping; if we wish to see the harvest, we must be willing to wait till the appointed time has come. History shows that in country after country missionaries have worked for about thirty years without seeing any result of their work. But, if they have gone on faithfully and not lost heart, after many years the results have come. In South India there was a mission which was known as the " Lone Star " Mission, because in thirty years of work it had won only one convert. Some thought that they ought to leave that area and go elsewhere. The missionaries met for prayer, and decided to go on a little longer in hope. Very soon after everything was changed. They had had no success with the higher caste people; but now suddenly the outcastes began to be interested in the Gospel. Where there had been only one convert, within a few years there were thousands, and a great Christian community was coming into being. If the missionaries had failed in patience and gone elsewhere, the time for reaping in that area would never have come.

Lastly, we need long patience, as we look out on the world, with all its evil, its strife and the constant danger of war. We are inclined to say, " Why doesn't God do something about it? " We may even begin to wonder whether God really is in charge of this world. We have a vivid picture of this state of mind in the New Testament in 2 Peter 3. The first Christians had thought that Jesus was very soon coming back to reign. When He did not come, they swung to the other extreme, and said, " Where is the promise of his coming? For ever since the fathers fell asleep, all things have continued as they were from the beginning of creation." St. Peter answers this in two ways. First, God does not look at time as we look at it (2 Peter 3 : 8). With Him a thousand years is as one day; we too must try to learn to look at time and at history with His eyes. If we look back even over a hundred years, can we not

see many signs of the work of Christ in the world—
in the ending of such evils as slavery, in greater freedom
for many nations and classes, in greater kindness of
men towards one another, in the spread of the Gospel
throughout the world? And, if we look around us
to-day, we shall see not only evil, but also many signs
that He is still at work. Secondly, says Peter, if God
does not at once come to judge evil, it is because He
wishes to give men time to repent (2 Peter 3 : 9). He
waits in order that through the Church the Gospel
may be preached to all nations. There is our task.
We do not know whether Christ will come at the end
of ten years, or a thousand, or ten thousand. That
is not our business. Our business is to wait patiently
for God to act in His own good time, and in the
meantime to get on with the work that He has given
us—the work of making Christ known to all men everywhere.

How are we to learn this virtue of patience? First,
by looking at Jesus Christ. He was never in a hurry.
How often He said " My hour has not yet come ".
He knew that He could not bring His message Himself to all men in the world; He was content to go
on in that little country of Palestine, each day doing
the work that came to Him that day, and leaving the
fruit of His sowing to be seen in God's good time.
Secondly, St. Paul tells us that patience is closely
connected with love (1 Cor. 13 : 4). Surely this is true.
If we love God, we shall be willing to trust Him, to
let Him work in His own way without trying to run
ahead of His will. If we love others, we shall not judge
them quickly or harshly. We shall bear with them when
they are unkind or fail to respond to our goodwill.
We shall be willing to wait until our love for them,
that is, God's love drawing near to them through us,

can have its effect, until the love of God draws them back to love.

We now begin to see that all the different Christian graces are connected with one another. Patience springs from love. The man who is impatient cannot have inner peace. The result of long patience is joy, when God allows us to see the reaping-time for which we have long waited, and which would never have come, unless we had been willing to await God's appointed time.

CHAPTER SIX

KINDNESS

Kindness is one of the ways in which love manifests itself: " Love is patient and kind " (1 Cor. 13 : 4; see also 2 Cor. 6 : 6). Everyone understands in general what the word means; we know quite well what it means to be kind to a dog or a cat, and such kindness is quite an important part of Christian conduct. But has the word some deeper meaning in the New Testament, such as will account for its inclusion among the specially Christian virtues?

Perhaps Luke 6 : 35 will carry us a long way towards understanding. Here kindness is spoken of as a part of the character of God Himself: " He is kind to the ungrateful and the selfish." It is natural to be kind to our friends, and to the members of our family. Kindness toward those who have deserved it is easy. Kindness toward those who are just helpless, like the stray cat that wants to sit by our fire, is not very hard. But this verse speaks of kindness to those who have not deserved it, in fact to those who have deserved the very opposite. This verse is in St. Luke's version of the Sermon on the Mount; if we look back to St. Matthew's version, we shall find the same thing set out even more plainly: " He makes his sun rise on the evil and on the good, and sends rain on the just and on the unjust " (Matt. 5 : 45). So, says our Lord, if the heavenly Father is like that, you must be like that too.

Here we have moved a step forward from the last chapter. In Old Testament times men had learned that God does not at once punish or destroy the sinner; He is patient and holds back His anger. Now we are told something further; so far from killing the sinner, God treats him kindly, gives him all the good things of the earth, satisfying his heart with food and gladness (Acts 14 : 17). Now it is always possible that men will fail to understand that it is God who gives all these good things; St. Paul complains of the stupid folk who " did not honour him as God or give thanks to him " (Romans 1 : 21; note the same idea as in Luke 6 : 35 above). But most simple people do recognize God's care for them. Ask a simple villager in India who it is who gives the rain; it is probable that he will point not to one of the many shrines of the lesser gods and spirits, but to the sky, and will utter the name of the one great God; all believe in that God, though they may not know much about Him, and may think of Him as being very far away. Now that science has shown us so many of what we call the natural causes of things, many people find it difficult to retain this simple faith in God as the giver of all good things. Yet clearly, in all our plans for making life better and safer, we can use only the good things that God has put into the world, and the minds that He Himself has given—we are still dependent upon God, and upon the kindness with which He rules the world.

But the Bible pays less attention than we do to the concerns of man's body. Man's spirit is so much more important; and his spiritual well-being depends on a right relationship to God. So twice over St. Paul uses the word we are studying to express the gentle, loving way in which God tries to bring back His children when they have strayed: " Do you presume upon the

53

riches of his kindness and forbearance and patience? Do you not know that God's kindness is meant to lead you to repentance?" (Romans 2 : 4). You cannot make men good by frightening them. You may make men afraid by punishing them, but you cannot make them sorry. The more men sinned, the more God showed His love and His kindness; until in the end He gave His Son as the last and only way of bringing man back to Himself. And so we find our word again in the Epistle to Titus; we were hateful, hating one another, but then "the *kindness*[1] and loving kindness of God our Saviour appeared" (Tit. 3 : 4).

The best commentary on this attitude of God is to be found in the beautiful courtesy of the father towards the elder son in the parable of the prodigal son. This son is a surly and unpleasant type. He is so full of his own righteousness that he is quite unable to feel any kindness towards the brother who has got into trouble. But his father came out and *entreated* him. That is a very remarkable word. In the days of Jesus, fathers usually just gave orders to their sons; but this father does not say to his son, "Come in at once"; he says, "Please come in; it will spoil the party if you don't." And then he adds, in words of melting tenderness, "Son, you are always with me, and all that is mine is yours." Did the father get what he wanted? We are not told, since that is where the parable ends. But what is remarkable is that St. Paul takes up exactly the same word—" So we are ambassadors for Christ, God making his appeal (entreating) through us. We beseech you on behalf of Christ, be reconciled to God." God entreats us. He doesn't say "You had better come home, or it will be the worse for you". He does say "Please come home; the party won't be complete without you".

[1] R.S.V. here translates the same Greek work by "goodness".

This picture of the kindness of God makes plain the kindness that will be expected of us, if we really want to be followers of Christ. We must think again of this question of being kind to the unthankful and the evil.

What do we do when someone has done us an injury? There are four possible ways of acting.

There is first just the plain simple method of taking the heaviest vengeance we can for every injury; of this there is a good example in the Old Testament, when the patriarch Lamech savagely cries out " I have slain a man for wounding me, a young man for striking me. If Cain is avenged sevenfold, truly Lamech seventy-sevenfold " (Gen. 4 : 23, 24).

The second level is that of " eye for eye, tooth for tooth " (Ex. 21 : 24). This is the way that ordinary human justice works; a man must pay for what he does. We do not now repay physical injury by physical injury, but the law tries to see to it that the punishment and the crime are roughly equal. This is a great advance on the unlimited vengeance that had gone before—it is only the rule of law that makes possible life in civilized societies. Sometimes even Christians have to set the law to work, not because they hate or are angry with the man who has done the wrong, but because it may be best for him and for everyone else that he should pay the penalty for the wrong that he has done.

The third level is that of bearing the evil that men do to us without trying to pay it back. This is very hard to do. The desire to defend ourselves, to hit back, is very strong indeed in all of us. " He has made me suffer; let him suffer in his turn." That is the way our minds work. It is not always easy to remember that we have a higher example to follow: " When he was reviled, he did not revile in return; when he suffered, he did

not threaten; but he trusted to him who judges justly "
(1 Peter 2 : 23).

But there is a yet higher level to which we must rise, if we are really to be the children of God. Not to do evil to others, when we could do it, is a great thing. But it is far better, when others have done us evil, to do them in return all the good that is in our power. This is something that we do not often see, and we do not often act this way ourselves. But it does happen when the Holy Spirit is at work. There is a touching story of a simple Christian in America at the time of the American Revolution, named Peter Miller. This good man had one enemy, who hated him so bitterly that he once went so far as to spit in his face. Miller bore this insult quietly and without any attempt to take revenge. Later, when the war with Britain began, Miller's enemy took the British side, and was said to have acted as a spy for the British. He was caught and sentenced to be hanged. Miller went to General Washington and begged him to spare the life of the condemned man. Washington replied that in such times it was necessary to deal most severely with spies and traitors: " otherwise," he added, " I should cheerfully release your friend." " Friend! " replied Miller, " he is the only enemy I have." Washington was so deeply impressed that he signed a pardon, and Miller arrived just in time to save his enemy.

Kindness demands that, when we have been injured, we should take the first step towards putting things right. This is hard to do; we tend to say " He has done the wrong; let him come and say that he is sorry." As he may have what seem to him good reasons for not saying that he is sorry, it may well come about that neither takes the first step, and so the wrong situation can never be put right. If we do decide to take the first step, we must be prepared to go all the way, as God has shown it to us. Once I was able with much difficulty to persuade a student to speak to someone whom he believed to have injured him, and to whom he had refused even to speak. But, when asked what he was going to say to him, he replied, " I want to tell him how wrong I think he has been." That is not what Christian kindness means. We are called to follow the example of God, who has taken the first step, and has come towards us in Jesus Christ, not holding out a long list of our sins, but pleading with us to be reconciled to Him.

We must be prepared for failure. If we could be sure that those whom we approach would respond to us, and that they would be sorry for the wrong that they had done, it would not be so difficult to act according to the law of kindness. But that is not the way the world is made. All that our Lord could do for Judas Iscariot could not turn him from his evil way. All the kindness that God shows to men does not make them thankful; many of them remain ungrateful still. What then are we to do? If a man who has done us wrong not merely is not sorry but even goes on to wrong us again, what are we to do with him? The answer of the Gospel is plain; we must go on forgiving him " until seventy times seven " (Matt. 18 : 22), that is without any limit to our willingness to forgive. We must not grow weary in our kindness. We must take as our example God, who is never weary of being kind to us.

Now perhaps we can understand some difficult sayings of our Lord: " If any one would sue you and take your coat, let him have your cloak as well," and " if any one forces you to go one mile, go with him two miles " (Matt. 5 : 40–41). It is not likely that either of these things will happen exactly to us, but what our

Lord's words mean for us is quite clear; in dealing with men, you have got to do all that anyone could possibly expect of you, and then some more. It is by that extra piece of service, which he could not possibly have claimed and which he does not expect, that you may be able to win his heart.

Our word for " kindness " is found in the New Testament in still one more unexpected place. " My yoke is *easy*, and my burden is light " (Matt. 11 : 30). The word " easy " in Greek is our same word " kind ". We have just been speaking of the terrible demands that Christ makes upon us, and the difficulty that we have in meeting them. How can we possibly say that His yoke is easy? Well, the Greek word may rightly be translated " well-fitting "; it is a yoke that does not gall the neck of the ox. If we will take His yoke upon us, we shall find that it is made just to fit us, that it suits exactly the true nature of man, as it is seen in Christ—that true nature, to which God wants to bring us all back. After all, does not our inmost heart tell us that Christ's way is the kind of way in which we really wish to live, even though we often find it so difficult? Perhaps if we accept His kind yoke, we shall find true what Samuel Rutherford said of the Cross: "He that will cannily carry that crabbit tree shall find it such a burden as wings are to a bird, or sails to a boat."

CHAPTER SEVEN

GOODNESS

It must seem strange to find *goodness* set down as one
of the forms of the fruit of the Spirit. Surely all these
virtues are goodness of one kind or another. Goodness
seems such a general word, and in fact it is often used
in the New Testament just as we use it in common
speech, as in the verse we have already quoted, that
God " makes his sun rise on the evil and on the good "
(Matt. 5 : 45). But, since St. Paul speaks of goodness
as one virtue among others, we may feel sure that he had
one special quality in mind; and, using the New Testament to guide us, we must try to find out what this is.[1]

It is interesting to note that two men only in the New
Testament are spoken of as being *good*. Joseph of
Arimathea was " a good and righteous man . . . and
he was looking for the kingdom of God " (Luke 23 :
50–51). Barnabas was " a good man, full of the Holy
Spirit and of faith " (Acts 11 : 24). Is there any quality
which these two men both possess, which will help us
to make clear the meaning of the word " goodness ",
as St. Paul uses it here?

We find that Joseph of Arimathea was sincere, and
that he was generous. He was a member of the Jewish
council but he had not agreed with the deed of the

[1] Note that there is another Greek word, which strictly means
"beautiful", but is translated "good" in such expressions as "I am
the good shepherd."

others in putting Jesus to death. It would have been easy for him to follow the opinion of others, and to vote as they did. But he was not that kind of man; he was one who wanted to watch things for himself, and to make up his own mind. Having made up his mind that Jesus was true, he would not change his mind because of the opinions of all the other councillors put together. He was generous. When Jesus was dead there was only one thing that he could give Him, and that was a tomb. He had a new tomb, cut out in the rock, where no human body had yet been laid (Luke 23 : 53, cf. Matt. 27 : 60). Probably he had prepared it for his own burial, and intended that his own body should be the first to lie in it. But when Jesus needs it, his own plans are forgotten, and the one thing that he can give to Jesus is gladly given.

The passage in which Barnabas is called " good " is a very interesting one. In the great city of Antioch some Christians had begun to preach to the Gentiles (Greeks). Some of these Gentiles had become Christians and had been baptized, but had not accepted any part of the old law of the Jews. When news of this reached Jerusalem, many questions were asked. The earliest Christians were all Jews, and most of them took it for granted that anyone who wanted to accept Christ must first accept the whole of the law of Moses as well. But now these Gentiles in Antioch were coming direct to Christ, without having anything to do with Moses. To all the strict Jews among the Christians this seemed terribly wrong. So Barnabas is sent down to Antioch to find out what is happening and to report upon it. Now Barnabas was not merely a Jew, he was also a Levite (Acts 4 : 36), of the priestly tribe. It seemed likely that he too would take a strict Jewish view, that he would say to those who were at work in Antioch,

" What you are doing is mistaken; all these new Gentile Christians must be circumcised, as a first step towards becoming Christians." But Barnabas also was a man who liked to look at things as they were, before making up his mind. He did not say, "What you are doing is quite different from what we have always done at Jerusalem; therefore it must be wrong." He lived among these new Christians; he became sure that they were true Christians, and that the grace of Christ was among them; having seen this, he reached the conclusion that God had done a new thing, and was glad: " When he came and saw the grace of God, he was glad " (Acts 11 : 23). He was prepared to look for the best in a situation, and to exercise a generous judgment upon it.

But we find that there was another way in which, like Joseph of Arimathea, Barnabas was generous. At a time when the Church in Jerusalem was in great need of money, Barnabas sold a field and brought the money and laid it at the apostles' feet (Acts 4 : 36–37). It looks as though the apostles had been going through a very bad time, wondering where the money was to come from for the next meal; since, when Barnabas brought in this money, they gave him a new name, the Son of encouragement—" the man who cheered us all up ", and that nickname stuck to him, so that his original name of Joseph came to be almost forgotten.

We have found a clue to the meaning of the word " goodness ", as part of the fruit of the Spirit. It is *generosity*—a necessary quality in anyone who wishes to be a servant of the Lord.

We have seen that one form of generosity is fair and kind and open-minded judgment of others. Some people are always ready to find fault. Others will always find something kind to say about everyone. Which of these characters is more like that of Jesus Christ? There is an

61

old story about our Lord, which is not found in any of the Gospels, and may not be true, but at least reflects something of His character. A number of people were standing round looking at a dead dog, and each had some cruel remark to make about the poor dead creature. But Jesus said, " Pearls cannot equal the whiteness of its teeth." We can often see in the Gospels that this was in fact the way in which He acted. Others could see only the bad side of a man; He saw the one point at which a man could be taken hold of in order to make him good. No one else would have believed that Zaccheus could be changed in a day from bad to good; our Lord saw and believed.

We cannot be the servants of Christ, unless we can learn to see people as He saw them. No doubt He was far more deeply aware than we can be of the evil that is in men; yet He never thought of any man as worthless, or as being beyond the reach of God's love. He always saw in them what He could make of them. It really is not much use telling people about their sins—after all they know a great deal more about them than we do. It is far more useful to see the very best that is in them, and to start to make friends with them at the point at which they are at their best. Even bad men love their children. But even if a man only keeps white mice and is kind to his mice—that ought to be enough to give us hope in the great things that God is able to do for him.

We, like Barnabas, need to look generously on new movements in the Church. In the history of the Church, we find that almost everyone who has ever tried to do something new has been condemned by those who think that the old is always better. Later, when the new movement has proved its worth, everyone is glad to praise it; our Lord Himself remarked that it was the habit of the

Jews first to kill the prophets and then to build their tombs. When John Wesley began to preach the Gospel with new power, he was forbidden by many of the clergy of the Church of England to preach in their churches; he took to preaching in the fields. When William Carey, the first great English missionary, who was a Baptist, set out to preach the Gospel in India, critics in England remarked that it was more likely that the Hindus would convert the Baptists than that the Baptists would convert the Hindus. Of course the new movement may be a bad movement; there have been many false prophets in the history of the Church, as well as many true prophets. But the good man does not judge in a hurry; he is willing to believe that God is able to do new things, and that sometimes He takes weak and simple people to do great things for Him.

Another field for generosity is the use of money. Barnabas sold his land, and brought the money and gave it to the apostles. There is one saying of our Lord in which the word " good " is used in this same sense of " generous ". It is in the parable of the labourers in the vineyard (Matt. 20 : 1–16). Some of the workmen had come at the end of the day, and had worked only one hour; and yet they received as much as the others, who had worked much longer. When one of those who had worked longer complained, the master of the vineyard says to him, " Is your eye evil because I am good? "[1]; that means: " Must you be mean, because I am generous? " The point is that the master has done a great deal more than he need have done. No one could have called him unjust, if he had paid the late-comers for only one hour's work. But this does not

[1] R.S.V. margin; R.S.V. text reads " Do you begrudge my generosity?"

63

seem right to him. After all, these men had not wanted to be idle, they had been willing to work; and they too, like the others, had wives and children waiting at home to be fed. The master acts generously, and sends them home with a wage that will make one more family happy for that day.

It is clear that our Lord approved of the generous heart, which is prepared to give without counting the cost. When a woman came and poured out a whole phial of precious ointment on His head, some of those who saw it said, " What a waste." But Jesus promised that, wherever in the world the Gospel was preached, what this woman had done would be told in memory of her (Matt. 26 : 6–13). As in so many stories in the Gospel, here a very simple action is seen to have a deeper inner meaning; here we are taught that those who wish to follow Christ must be willing to give themselves wholly to Him, without delay and without keeping anything back for themselves.

The right use of money is not the most important of Christian virtues. Yet it is an important virtue, and it is astonishing how few Christians pay careful attention to it. Sometimes we are called to sudden acts of great generosity, like that of Barnabas who sold his land. But more often what God wants of us is a steady attitude of responsibility, which accepts everything that we have as a gift from God, and uses the whole of it as in His sight. This can be done only if we pay attention to details, and regard watchfulness in the use of money as a serious Christian duty.

Very few Christians keep careful accounts. They know more or less how much money they have had, and how much they have spent. But, if for a month they were to keep exact account of where the money had gone to, they would be astonished to see how much they had spent on themselves, and how little had gone to help others or to carry on the work of God.

Some Christians spend more than they earn, and, when bills come in, find that they have not the money with which to pay them. Others are careless, and when the day comes on which bills ought to be paid, are inclined to say, " To-morrow will do just as well." Surely both these attitudes show a failure in the sense of responsibility. If we love God, we should be able to trust Him to give us all that He sees we really need. If we love our neighbour, we should not keep back from him for a single day that which is due to him.

It is only when we are willing to accept the Christian rule of responsibility in the sight of God that we are able to be generous with our money. When we know exactly how much we have and how we spend it, we shall be astonished to find how much we are able to give away to others who are in need. We are not under the old Jewish law, and we are not required to fix any special proportion of our income to give to God or to use in the service of others. And now in most countries there is a new problem; taxes are so heavy, and the state does so much—education, medical care and so on—that used to be done by private charity that people find it difficult to decide how much they should give. But those who decide to follow the old Jewish law and regularly to give a tenth (which may now perhaps be a tenth of what they have left after all taxes are paid) often find that they can give this amount without too grave a sacrifice, and that the giving of it brings them much happiness.

At present no part of the work of the Church has enough money. Whether it is building new churches in Christian countries, or carrying on missionary work which has already been started, or going out into new lands where the Gospel has never been preached, never is there enough money to do what needs to be done. There is plenty of money in the world and in the pockets of Christians; but it does not get to the right place. But once again let us remember that the Christian generosity of which we are here speaking is a fruit of the Spirit. The writer, in his ministry, has found it an excellent rule never to ask people directly for money. Naturally, Christians should be taught the principles of Christian Giving. Naturally, they must be told where the needs are. But what they do about it is a matter between them and their conscience in the sight of God. Bring people to Christ. Teach them to let the Holy Spirit rule in their hearts. Then it will be impossible to stop them giving, and what is needed for the Lord's work will be found.

CHAPTER EIGHT

FAITHFULNESS

The Greek word here translated " faithfulness " in the R.S.V. must in many other passages be translated " faith ". But here most modern translations render " faithfulness "—and it is almost certain that they are right. Faith is the starting-point of the Christian life. But, in the earlier chapters of this Epistle, Paul has spoken at length about this faith; now he is talking about the unfolding of Christian character through the work of the Spirit. There is no need for him at this point to go back and speak of faith in that earlier sense; here he is showing us, not the man who trusts in God, but the man *who can be trusted*: that is the meaning of faithfulness.

If we are called to learn this virtue, it is because in learning it we shall become like God Himself. Again and again in the Bible, God is spoken of as the faithful God, the God whom men can trust, because He is true. " He who calls you is faithful, and he will do it," says St. Paul (1 Thess. 5 : 24); and again " God is faithful, and he will not let you be tempted beyond your strength " (1 Cor. 10 : 13). This idea runs right through both Old and New Testaments.

God is faithful, in the sense that He is true to Himself. He does not act now on one principle and now on another; He never changes. " If we are faithless, he remains faithful—for he cannot deny himself " (2 Tim. 2 : 13).

He is faithful, in the sense that He is true to His word; if He has made a promise, He can be relied on to keep it. When the people of Israel looked back over their own history, they saw that this was true: " Not one of all the good promises which the Lord had made to the house of Israel had failed; all came to pass " (Jos. 21 : 45).

He is faithful in the sense that He is true to His people; He will never give up or forsake those whom He has chosen: " He has said, ' I will never fail you nor forsake you '. Hence we can confidently say, ' The Lord is my helper, I will not be afraid; what can man do to me? ' " (Heb. 13 : 5, 6).

Because God is true, man can trust Him. The great example of this trust is Abraham. He had received a promise that a son would be born to him when he was old. Everything seemed to make this unlikely, but Abraham was " fully convinced that God was able to do what he had promised " (Rom. 4 : 21). Sarah " considered him faithful who had promised " (Heb. 11 : 11), and so through faith received the fulfilment of the promise. What had Abraham to rest on? Nothing but the promise of God, but for him that was enough; he believed, and in due time God showed that He was true to His word: Isaac was born and the promise was fulfilled.

We can count on God. Through the work of the Spirit in us, we are to grow into the kind of people who can be trusted. God must be able to count on us to do honestly the work that He gives us to do. Others should be able to count on us to keep our word, to work hard, to be in every way reliable.

This quality is often spoken of in the New Testament. " It is required of stewards that they be found faithful " (" trustworthy ", R.S.V.) (1 Cor. 4 : 2). It is no stated that the steward must be either clever or successful; it is said that he must be *faithful*. Whom would you choose to manage your affairs? Surely the man you can trust to do what he is told, and to care for his master's interests rather than for his own. In the parable of the talents, the two servants who had received money from their lord, and had used it wisely while he was away, were praised because they had been *faithful*; each had done what he could; each gave back honestly to the master what he had gained in his name. So each is praised: " Well done, good and faithful servant; you have been faithful over a little, I will set you over much; enter into the joy of your master " (Matt. 25 : 21). In warning His disciples about the danger of carelessness, our Lord uses once again the same word: " Who then is the faithful and wise servant, whom his master has set over his household? " (Matt. 24 : 45).

We do not have to look far around us in the world to see how true to life the New Testament teaching is. Who is the man whom others want to employ? The first question about a man may be, " Is he clever? ", but the second and much more important question is, " Can we trust him? " Probably we have all at one time or another heard the head of a big business concern pay this kind of tribute to one of his clerks: " Of course I am not really the important person here. So-and-so does all the important work. He is always in his place on time. He always knows everything that is going on. He never thinks of himself, but always of the interests of the firm. You never have to watch him to see whether he is working or not, and there is no secret with which you cannot trust him. I simply don't know what we should do without him." Happily there are many such people in the world. And it ought to be possible to take it for granted that, if a man is a Christian, all those things will be true of him.

There are a great many Christians of whom all those things are true. If it were not so, the Church would long ago have ceased to exist. How does the Church go on from age to age? In each century there are a few outstanding Christians whose names get into the history books. But much more important than these few are the many of whom no one ever hears; those who went on faithfully and quietly serving God, without ever losing heart and without ever asking for a reward. Every Sunday the minister will be in church to take the services. Sometimes many people come to church, sometimes only a few; sometimes no-one comes at all. But the minister is always there. And we sometimes forget the other faithful people who go on year after year serving the Church—sextons who keep the churches clean; organists who never fail to be there to play for services; members of choirs who come Sunday after Sunday. It is through such people that the life of the Church is carried forward. Sometimes they have to carry on through many years in which very little seems to happen. But they know that God is faithful, and that He uses the faithfulness of men to carry out His great purpose for the world.

In addition to loyalty to the Church, there are three main ways in which the faithfulness of the Christian should be shown.

First, we should be able to go on quietly in good times and in bad, without ever losing heart. It is impossible that life should always be easy and pleasant; the times of sorrow and suffering will come. If we have learned that God is faithful, and that His faithfulness is like a strong rock, we shall be able to trust in Him, and our faithfulness to Him will be our response to His faithfulness to us.

Secondly, we must be faithful in the unseen duties of private prayer and Bible-reading. Why is the cause of Christ so weak in the world to-day? Where is it being defeated? Surely the answer is that one place of defeat is in the homes and lives of Christians. It ought to be so easy to be faithful in such simple matters. But we all know by experience how difficult it is. The majority of those who call themselves Christians never really pray at all. Very few give even as much as ten minutes a day to God. Then we are surprised that we do not make progress in the Christian life, that we are weak in the moment of temptation. Until we are faithful in this matter, we cannot even begin to make progress in the other virtues which make up the Christian life.

Thirdly we must be faithful in service. We must be the kind of people of whom others will say, " You can always count on that man; you can always trust him, he will never let you down." This must be true in daily life, in the place of our work and in our homes. It must specially be true in our Christian service. To take just one point out of many; we must be the kind of people to whom others can easily talk, knowing that everything they tell us will be safe with us. It is astonishing how few people can keep a secret. Christians, even ministers, too often fail in this easy and obvious duty. To be able to hear all and say nothing is the first rule for those who would be good servants of their Master.

From what we have said it may seem that faithfulness is a very dull virtue. It just means going on day after day doing the same old things, without seeing very much as a result of what we do. Yes; but God's world is never really dull. We never know what may happen

71

to-morrow or even to-day. Moses went on for a very long time feeding the flocks of his father-in-law in the desert. That must have seemed very dull after living like a prince in Egypt. But one day the word of the Lord came to him, saying, " Go back into Egypt and set my people free." David was only a shepherd boy. The only exciting thing that ever happened to him was that sometimes he had a fight with wild beasts. But one day the call came to him to go back to his father's house, and there he found Samuel waiting to tell him that he was to be king over the people of God. Our Lord Himself went on for long years in the carpenter's shop, where nothing much ever happened. But, when the right time came, the Holy Spirit came down upon Him at His baptism, and sent Him forth to His work. Most of us will not be called to do anything great for God. And yet, in this troubled world of ours, we never know to what we may be called. The Churches in Germany had lived a very peaceful life for many years. Then suddenly, when the Nazis came to power, Christians found that, if they were true to Christ, they might be faced with cruel suffering and perhaps even with death. They heard the word of Christ, " Be faithful unto death, and I will give you the crown of life " (Rev. 2 : 10). Many pastors were put to death by the Nazis. Many more died in concentration camps. Hundreds will bear in their bodies till the end of their lives the marks of the sufferings of those days. In Japan during the war, many Christians found that to be true to Christ might expose them to the charge of disloyalty to their country. Some proved weak and chose wrong: many proved strong and chose right. The Churches in Germany and Japan are rightly proud of those who were willing to suffer all things for Christ and His Name.

When we are young, we are inclined to say, " If

only Christ would give me some great thing to do for Him, I would gladly do it." But it is certain that those who are careless in small things will not be found fit for great ones. Only those who have been faithful in the small tasks of every day will be found ready and faithful when the moment of great opportunity or great trial comes. It is the Lord's own word: " He who is faithful in a very little is faithful also in much " (Luke 16 : 10). And God does not measure great and small as we measure them. He who watches over the sparrows is aware of all that we do, and our faithfulness in small things is precious in His sight.

CHAPTER NINE

GENTLENESS

The Greek word for the virtue which we now have to consider is here translated " gentleness " in the R.S.V.; but in a number of other passages the R.S.V. translates " meekness "; and I may frankly express my opinion that it is a great pity that, although the word " meekness " is rather out of fashion, the R.S.V. has not retained the older translation in every place where the word occurs.

There are two words in the New Testament which seem to mean nearly the same thing—humility and meekness. They are found together in Ephesians 4 : 2 and Colossians 3 : 12.

Here again we must note that the New Testament writers have put into these words a meaning different from that which they had in the older Greek language. To the Greeks, the word which we translate " humble " meant something more like " mean, poor-spirited "; it is used of the man who has not enough courage to stand up for himself. The Greeks regarded this as a bad quality. But the Christian character which we are studying is not the same as the ideal of the good man which men had before Christ came into the world. Christ has given us a quite new idea of what a man ought to be; to put this new idea into words, we need new words or old words which are filled with new meaning.

Our Lord uses both these words of Himself in Matthew 11 : 29: " I am meek and lowly (humble) in heart." Can we find a difference in meaning between the two words?

Perhaps " humble " speaks of what a man ought to be before God. What was man's first and great sin? He wanted to be like God (Genesis 3 : 5). He wanted to be free from God, to be his own god. Would we not all like to have a world of our own, in which everything happens just as we want it to happen, and in which everything is subject to our will? This is exactly the opposite of what we should be; we have to learn to live in the world as God made it, and honestly to accept God as God. That is what it means to be humble. There are two steps in humility; the first is to know that we cannot do anything without God. The second is not to want to do anything without God.

In this, as in all things, the Son of God is our great example. St. John's Gospel is the Gospel of the glory of Christ. Yet what is the picture of Himself which our Lord gives in this Gospel? Three times over He says: " On my own authority I can do nothing " (John 5 : 19, 30; 8 : 28). He says " I have not come of my own accord " (John 7 : 28). He says " I have not spoken on my own authority " (John 12 : 49). At all times He knows what to say, because at all times He is listening for the Father's word. He knows when to act and what to do, because He is at all times obedient to the will of God. He knows that He can do all things, because He claims no power for Himself, but can at every moment receive all the power that He needs from the Father.

This is the way in which men too must learn to live. But this word " humility " is not found in St. Paul's list of Christian virtues. Perhaps this is because humility

75

is not really *one* of the Christian virtues; it is that quality without which no Christian virtue can exist. Plants cannot grow without nitrogen. Christian character cannot grow without humility. Unless we are right at this point, unless we really accept God as God, it is useless to talk about growth in Christian character.

If " humility " is the right attitude to God, perhaps " meekness " is the right attitude towards men. As we have seen, Christ says that He Himself is meek (Matt. 11 : 29). He also pronounces a special blessing on the meek: " Blessed are the meek, for they shall inherit the earth " (Matt 5 : 5). We may say, to put it briefly, that the meek are those who do not resist the wrong that other men do to them, and do not insist on their own rights.

This is set out for us very plainly in one of the shortest and simplest stories in the Gospels. Jesus was on His way to Jerusalem for the last time. He wished to spend the night in a village of the Samaritans, but they would not receive Him. James and John, the sons of thunder, wanted to call down fire from heaven to destroy them. But Jesus rebuked them, and they went on to another village (Luke 9: 52–56).

We are all like James and John. If anyone is rude to us or injures us, we burn with anger. We feel that we must teach them a lesson; we must show them that they cannot do this kind of thing and get away with it. Perhaps it is just as well that we cannot call down fire from heaven, as Elijah is reported to have done (2 Kings 1 : 9–15), or there might not be many people left in the world.

Now look at the attitude of Jesus. " They went on to another village." That is all. He would not press in on those who did not want Him. They ought to have received Him; to break the law of hospitality in this way was a serious matter. But He would not insist on His rights. And what is the result? It seems as though the Samaritans had won; they have driven away the unwanted guest. But what is the inner reality? They have lost for ever their chance of having the Son of God among them. This attitude of our Lord is seen even more clearly and perfectly in the whole story of the Cross. This is how St. Peter sums it up for us: " When he was reviled, he did not revile in return; when he suffered, he did not threaten; but he trusted to him who judges justly " (1 Peter 2 : 23).

It is hard for Christians to believe that this really is the rule by which they must live. When they are harmed by their neighbours, it is very natural for them to think that they should call in the authorities, assert their rights, and get the matter put right by law. But what happens if they do so? I can speak only from experience in India. In old days, when the Christians were persecuted, the missionaries used often to go to law on their behalf. If the Christians won their case, there would be no more trouble and they would be able to live in peace with their neighbours. But after that no Hindu in that village would ever become a Christian. The victory of the Christians had made a spiritual barrier which perhaps in sixty years no one ever crossed. The Christians seemed to have won; but they had lost out in the all-important thing—the opportunity to win others in their village for Christ.

When people are suffering from the wrong done by others, it is very hard for them to believe that the best thing for them to do is to bear witness for Christ by enduring the suffering patiently. " But if they will not let us draw water from the village well, how can we live in this village? We have a right to draw water; they have no right to stop us." All depends on how far we are willing to trust God, and to believe that He will find a way out, even when we can see no way. It does sometimes happen that, when we do not demand our full rights, we gain more in the end than if we had stood up for ourselves. When we are willing to be meek, our gentleness does help others to be gentle too; whereas our saying, " We must have justice " may only make them harder than they were before.

If we study the teaching of Christ on this subject, we shall find that it does not fit in well with what most men believe. The world to-day is full of talk about *rights*. Charters of human rights are being drawn up; the nations are trying to agree on what these rights are, and how they are to be safeguarded. This is on the whole a good thing. But we have to ask ourselves whether the idea of the rights of man is a Christian idea or not.

In the Anglican Catechism, children learn about their duty to God and their duty to their neighbour. But they learn nothing about their rights. Is the Catechism right in putting things this way? Would it be true to say that the Bible teaching is that everyone else has *rights*, but I have only *duties*? To put it another way, I must never ask anything for myself (except that I may learn to be more like Christ); I must never seek to defend myself against wrong. But I must at all times be willing to die for the sake of others; I must be willing to pay any price in the defence of their rights. Christ spoke in very strong terms of the rights of children, of the duty of all men to care for them, and of the terrible judgment that would come on those who injured them (Matt. 18 : 1–14). But He never sought anything for Himself. He gave Himself for others; it was true that He saved others, because He could not save Himself.

Clearly, if we accept this as our rule of life, the principles on which we shall act will be quite different from those of other men of good will. And most of them will say that it is impossible to live in this way in such a world as ours. But St. Paul follows up exactly the teaching of Christ. Some of the Christians in Corinth had been going to law with one another. Paul tells them that this is wrong in any case, even if they had kept the quarrels within the Church, instead of carrying them outside to judges who were not Christians. " Why not rather suffer wrong? why not rather be defrauded? " (1 Cor. 6 : 7). " But we couldn't do that. He has my money, hasn't he? How am I to live, if I don't get it back? " The answer to this point of view is given in a beautiful little story in the Old Testament. A king of Judah thought that his army was not large enough, so he sent a hundred talents of silver to the king of Israel to hire other soldiers with. But a prophet came and told him not to use the soldiers of Israel, because God would not be with them. " And Amaziah said to the man of God, ' But what shall we do about the hundred talents which I have given to the army of Israel? ' The man of God answered, ' The Lord is able to give you much more than this ' " (2 Chron. 25 : 9).

St. Peter tells us of another sphere in which the virtue of meekness must be seen: " Always be prepared to make a defence to any one who calls you to account for the hope that is in you, yet do it with gentleness (meekness) and reverence " (1 Peter 3 : 15). Why does he speak of meekness in connection with Christian witness? The opposite of meekness is wanting to get the better of someone else, wanting to impose our will on a situation. Is not this exactly the way in which we sometimes give our Christian witness? We make others feel that what we want is to set ourselves up and to put them down. Naturally they do not like it. It is easy to win an argument and to lose a man. Often it is far better not to say, " I will tell you the truth; now listen ", but to say, " Tell me how it looks to you." If we are willing to listen to others, perhaps when the time comes for us to speak, we shall find them willing to listen.

This is specially important in dealing with young people. Young people have many doubts and questions. Ask them why they do not go to their minister for help, and they may give one or all of the following answers: " He will be angry with us for having these doubts "; " He won't understand what we are talking about "; " He will give us answers which are no real answers to our questions." Young people will come to older friends only if they are sure that they will be listened to with respect, and that they will be given honest answers to their questions. Some ministers are afraid of saying that they do not know; they think that they will lose the respect of those who have asked the question. A meek man is never afraid; if he is asked a question to which he does not know the answer, he will say quite simply, " I don't know, but let us try and find out together." There is much magic in those two little words " let us ".

It is difficult to be meek. We all like to have our own way. If we have been given authority, we like to use it. A father has authority in his family. A teacher has authority in his school. A minister has authority in his parish. Certainly each must use that authority, but each must use it in the right way. The danger always is that he may use it only to assert his own will. But, if we act in this way, we are not following Christ. Consider what is said of Him in the New Testament. He took upon Him " the form of a servant " (Phil. 2 : 7) This simply takes up one of the greatest of all our Lord's own sayings: " Let the greatest among you become as the youngest, and the leader as one who serves. . . . I am among you as one who serves" (Luke 22 : 26–27). St. Paul speaks in exactly the same terms of his own work: "What we preach is not ourselves, but Jesus Christ as Lord, with ourselves as your servants for Jesus' sake. . . . Not that we lord it over your faith; we work with you for your joy" (2 Cor. 4 : 5; 1 : 24). As long as we want to be masters, we cannot become like Christ. It is only when we are willing to be servants to all men that His likeness begins to be seen in us.

CHAPTER TEN

SELF-CONTROL

The Greek word for our last virtue is translated
" temperance " in the English Authorized Version,
but " self-control " in the Revised Standard Version.
There is no doubt that this second translation is the
better. Temperance is a fine word. But in modern
English it is often used in a very narrow sense—
abstinence from alcoholic drinks. This is a pity. We
must firmly resist the view that by *not* doing certain
things we shall become good Christians. Each of our
great Christian words is much more concerned with
what we must do than with what we must not do; to
be a Christian is a positive and not a negative thing.

In the time of our Lord and of St. Paul, there were
groups of people called Essenes, who lived a very strict
life, and tried to be holy by refusing to do a great many
things which other people did. An old Jewish writer,
Josephus, describes them in the following terms:
" Pleasures they reject as being an evil; self-control
and not yielding to desire they regard as virtue." In all
ages many Christians have held a view something like
this. There is a famous saying of an historian about
certain Christians in England who wished to put a stop
to the cruel sport of bull-baiting; he says that they
disliked it, not because it gave pain to the bull, but
because it gave pleasure to the spectators. I once heard
a famous man say that he was brought up by strict

Christian grandparents on the principle that, if there was anything that the children liked, that was what the children should not have.

This is not true Christianity. It starts from a false view about God and about ourselves. Almost the first thing we are told in the Bible is that " God saw everything that he had made, and behold, it was very good " (Gen. 1: 31). But the world is not as it was when God made it. Sin has entered in and spoiled the good work of God. In some ways we are like a machine that has gone out of order, and in which the parts are no longer working together in harmony. In men desire is no longer subject to the spirit. In seeking to be free, we often find that we have really lost our freedom, and have become the slaves of habits that we know to be bad and of ideas that we know to be false.

Since it is with our bodies that we act, the poor body often gets a lot of blame which it does not deserve. In the time of St. Paul, the Greeks thought that the body was itself bad and evil—the prison, in which the soul has somehow got shut up. The soul should have as little to do with the body as possible; that is the only way for it to be saved. Now it is true that the body acts, and says and does evil things. But what makes it act? Where does the sin really come from? It is clear that sin comes from within us, just as our Lord said (Mark 7 : 20–23). We think of evil things. We let our minds be infected by desires that we know to be wrong. Then the evil desire acts on the will and leads it to make a wrong choice. The will directs the tongue or the hand to act, and the evil word is spoken or the evil deed is done. Every time we sin, it is the whole of us that sins and not just a part. The body is only the instrument of the mind and the will. All that God made, including the body with all its desires and instincts, is good in itself. But it has to be kept under control and used in the right way.

The origin of sin is nearly always a wrong choice. It is the wrong use of something that in itself is good, and will always be good when used in the right way. If what is good is used in the wrong time, in the wrong place, and in the wrong way, of course sin will result. This will become clear, if we think of the prodigal son in our Lord's parable. The young man was heir to part of his father's possessions. But he would not wait till the right time, namely, after his father's death. He said, " I must have it now." So he went astray in the matter of time. Having received the inheritance he went away into a far country. This was the error of place; he ought to have stayed at home. He used it in the wrong way. An inheritance is given as a trust. What the young man received should have been used to keep the farm and the fields in good order, and to build up the life of the family. Instead he used it selfishly just for his own pleasure.

This is not true of all sins, e.g., lying or cruelty. But it is true of a great many. One instinct which a great many men and women find difficult to control is the instinct of sex. So much so that there has grown up even among Christians, an idea that this instinct is in itself bad. Of course this is nonsense. It is easy to see where wrong and evil come in; the instinct is and remains holy, if it is rightly used in relation to time and place and manner. All is well, if we will wait till the right time comes, that is, until the instinct is made holy by the pure love of one man for one woman and one woman for one man. All is well, if the instinct acts only in the right place, that is in the home, the centre of lifelong union of two people who love one another. All is well if it is used in the right manner, not selfishly

84

but for the building up of a family, in which parents and children love one another and love God. All is well, if it is used not simply as the demand of a man upon a woman, but with restraint, and with mutual respect of husband for wife and wife for husband.

All New Testament teaching on self-control is much more concerned with what we are to do than with what we are not to do. Let us consider two points on which St. Paul lays special emphasis:

(1) God is concerned with the whole of us, and the whole of us is to be given to God for His service. He prays for his friends that God will sanctify them wholly, and that the whole man, spirit and soul and body, may be kept sound and blameless at the coming of our Lord Jesus Christ (1 Thess. 5 : 23). He tells us that our bodies are the temple of the Holy Spirit (1 Cor. 6 : 19). He specially tells us to present our bodies a living sacrifice to God (Rom. 12 : 1).

(2) No one can use his body wrongly without harming others; but since we belong to one another, since we are all members in one body, to harm others is equally to harm ourselves (see the whole passage Eph. 4 : 17–5 : 33). If someone says, " If I drink too much, is that not my own affair? ", the answer quite clearly is, " No ". We need go no further than the daily papers to see how many accidents are caused on the roads by men and women driving cars when under the influence of drink. Among Christians such things must not be. For our own sake and for the sake of others, we must learn to rule ourselves.

If we had never sinned, we should find this easy. Because we have sinned, we have to learn self-control by the hard way of *discipline*; and to most of us this presents itself as unpleasant.

Millions of young men to-day have had experience

of discipline in the armed services. It has seemed to them that the one aim of this discipline was to crush men, to teach them to behave like machines. If discipline has this result, of course it is bad and harmful. But the real purpose to which discipline in an army is directed is quite different. Its aims are (1) to make it possible for large bodies of men to move quickly, so that forces can be moved rapidly wherever they are needed; (2) to create the sense of loyalty among comrades, so that men will not fail their friends in the day of battle; (3) to strengthen men's wills to hold on when they are utterly tired and worn out. It is by the last five minutes of endurance that battles are won.

It is easy to see how these principles apply in the warfare of the Church against evil, and in our own inner war against sin. Especially the third. When we fail, others see only the failure; perhaps there has been a long struggle of which they have seen nothing; and perhaps an extra five minutes of strength to resist would have brought us victory instead of failure.

Everywhere in the New Testament we shall find the emphasis on this positive purpose of discipline. St. Paul speaks of those who are in training for the great athletic games: " Every athlete exercises self-control in all things " (1 Cor. 9 : 25). We know well to-day what strict rules regarding food and drink and sleep must be observed by those taking part in any great athletic contest. But all these rules have a positive purpose— that on the day of the contest a man may have all his powers fully at his disposal, to be used in the best possible way to win him the victory. So, says St. Paul, I am stern with myself; not because I despise my body, but because I honour it; not because I hate my body, but because I want to be able to use it to the full in the service of my Lord (1 Cor. 9 : 27).

Every man ought to be master in his own house; he cannot be master if he is pulled this way and that by desires that he cannot control. Every Christian is called to serve God with all his powers; he cannot do so if all the time he is fighting a civil war within himself. How then are we to learn the art of ruling ourselves? How are we to develop this, the last of our nine Christian virtues?

First, let us be clear that making good resolutions does not help. A resolution is an act of the will. It is just because our wills are weak that we so often fail.

Second, let us be clear that this fortress cannot be taken by direct assault. With many temptations, the only result of trying to fight them directly is to increase their power. We have to find another way to get round behind them and so to rob them of their power.

Self-control is a work of the Spirit. We shall gain it by letting the Holy Spirit rule our hearts and our thoughts. By far the most important step is to have each day a quiet time, in which we set ourselves to seek the power of the Holy Spirit. It is good in such times just to sit quiet, to open ourselves as fully as we can to the influence of the Holy Spirit, and let Him take control of thought and will, of action and desire.

If we find self-control difficult in big things, let us start with small things. Many people complain that they cannot control their thoughts when they pray. The right question to ask such people is, " How many things in a day do you really do with the whole of your mind and attention? " Most things we do with only half our minds. Is it surprising that, when we pray, we pray with only half our minds? It is simple and very useful to set ourselves every day to do certain simple things with the whole of our minds. When you write a letter, do you give the whole of your mind to writing in such a way that every letter is perfectly formed and perfectly easy to read? Many Christians and ministers have untidy work-tables. Time is wasted hunting for letters and papers, because we have not taken the trouble to put them in the right place when they arrived. Is our soul likely to be tidier than our table? And is keeping our table tidy perhaps good practice for keeping our souls in order too?

These are small things—as small as the endless little tasks that a soldier has to do. But why has he to do them? Because he belongs to an army, with thousands of companions, who must be able to count on him in the hour of danger. The long months of discipline and training seem to have very little meaning; their purpose is seen and tested in the day of battle. What we are called to is something far greater than the career of a soldier. We are called to take sides with God in His vast conflict against all the forces of evil in the world. We are called to stand loyally side by side with all the great company of Christians in the world. They are counting on us. If we fail, they will all be the weaker for our failure. God is counting on us: He depends on men to win His victories in the world.

Who can fight in such a conflict? Only the man who is at peace within himself. Only the man whose powers and capacities are all under his control. Only the man who is utterly loyal to the cause and utterly forgetful of himself. Where is such a man to be found? There has been only one such man—Jesus Christ. How can we become such men? Only as Jesus Christ dwells in our hearts by faith. And how can this happen? This is the gift of the Holy Spirit, whom Jesus has sent to be with us and to dwell with us for ever.

WHAT CAN I DO ABOUT IT?

The reader who has read so far may be inclined to say, " I know that that is what I ought to be like. But I am not like that. What am I to do? " The answer that we shall find in many books on the Christian life is " Pray more and try harder."

The first part of this answer may well be right; we never can pray enough. The second part is likely to be quite wrong. The Christian life is not something that we can get by trying to get it. If I am not joyful, can I make myself joyful just by trying to be joyful? Will not the result be that I shall pretend to be joyful, while all the time inside I am even sadder than before? If so, I shall be under great strain; and, if I am under strain, I certainly shall not have peace, the third of the Christian virtues that we have studied.

Very often the correct answer to the question is, " Stop trying on your own account, and let God act. Learn to receive before you try to give." All through we have reminded ourselves that this Christian life is the fruit of the Spirit. These Christian graces are gifts that we are to receive from God and to use to His glory. The Holy Spirit is far more willing to give than we are to receive. If we are not receiving these gifts from Him, that can only be because we are hindering Him, we are resisting His will. If we will stop hindering Him, He will be able to act; and then the fruit of His action will begin to be seen in us.

How do we hinder Him? This has come out plainly in some of our earlier studies. We want to have our own way. We want to make our own plans. We want to rule ourselves. We are tempted to commit again the sin of Adam and Eve, and to claim independence of God. Many people are discontented with the place in which God has put them and with the work that He has given them to do. But to-day I can be only where I am; to-day I can be only what I am. To-morrow God may tell me to go to some quite different place. To-morrow, by His help, I may be better than I am to-day. But if to-day I am wishing that I was somewhere else, I am hindering Him from meeting me where I am. If to-day I am wishing that I was someone else, I am hindering Him from giving me the help that I need to-day, just because I am what I am and not something or someone else. When I am willing to be where I am and what I am and as I am, here and now Christ can meet me and say to me again, " Follow me."

Let us always remember that the only place in which we can learn to live as Christians is in our daily life and our daily work. Our morning time of prayer is very important, since it is there that we prepare ourselves for what we have to do each day. Our evening time of prayer is very important, since it is there that we look back and see where we have failed. But life is always lived with other people; whether we are Christians or not can be seen in the way that we live with others. Love is not kind thoughts. It means acting lovingly towards the other members of our family, towards those whom we meet every day in our place of work, to those whom we meet by chance just once. Meekness is not a virtue that we can exercise by ourselves. It is shown in our attitude to others, and especially in the way that we feel towards them and act towards them when they have hurt us or done us an injury.

It is essential to be quite honest with ourselves, to see quite clearly where we have failed, and not to cover up our failures. It is not enough just to remember the wrong action done or the wrong word spoken. We have to ask ourselves why we did wrong, to look back and note the point at which we began to go wrong. We must not try to put the blame on others, or on the devil, or on some specially strong temptation. We shall always find that the true answer is the same. The law of the Christian life is plainly set out by St. Paul in the words, " It is no longer I who live, but Christ who lives in me " (Gal. 2 : 20). Our Lord puts the same law in the words, " Abide in me, and I in you . . . apart from me you can do nothing " (John 15 : 4–5). If we have failed, it can only be because we were not abiding in Him. We have moved off our centre in Him. With His help we must get back to that centre; otherwise we shall continue to fail in exactly the same way.

This means that we must develop the habit of always looking towards Christ. He is the only one who has ever lived the perfect life. It is only through looking at Him, studying over and over again His life as we have it set out in the Gospels, directing our thoughts to Him many times in the day, that we can learn what it means to live as God wishes us to live. We must not try to copy Christ; we could not, even if we wished to. We shall not always get help even by asking, " What would Christ have done if He had been in this situation? " Our life to-day is so different from that of His time, and there are so many new problems, that we cannot always get a direct answer. There are times when we shall not know how to act. It is certain

91

that, however sincere and humble we are, we shall sometimes make mistakes. But it is certain that, as we keep our minds fixed on Christ and His life, we shall come to understand ever more clearly what kind of people we ought to be, and in every situation what kind of decisions we ought to make. Jesus promised that the Holy Spirit " will take what is mine and declare it to you " (John 16 : 14). As that living Spirit lights up the words and deeds of Christ for us, they become a living light, a living message for us to-day.

Let us never be troubled if we do not feel that we are growing into the likeness of Christ. We have said it before; let us say it again. We shall not feel that we are growing. The growth of our bodies took place without our even noticing that it was happening, until suddenly we realized that we could see over the wall that a few months before had been too high for us. It is the same in the growth of our spirits—*if* we remain rooted in Christ and learn to grow as the trees and the flowers do. We shall always know the evil that is in our hearts, and that will keep us humble. But if we are trying to follow Christ and to let the Holy Spirit work, others will see the change in us, and they will thank God for it. It is only when the Holy Spirit has finished His work in us that we shall be allowed to see what He has done. Then we shall be astonished to see how gently He has led us, how patient He has been with all our failures. In the meantime we can hold fast to the great promise that " when he appears we shall be like him, for we shall see him as he is " (1 John 3 : 2).